OSPREY COMBAT AIRCRAFT • 86

TYPHOON WINGS OF 2ND TAF 1943-45

SERIES EDITOR: TONY HOLMES

OSPREY COMBAT AIRCRAFT • 86

TYPHOON WINGS OF 2ND TAF 1943-45

CHRIS THOMAS

OSPREY
PUBLISHING

Front cover
Sqn Ldr B G 'Stapme' Stapleton, a Battle of Britain Spitfire ace and the man who shot down Franz von Werra, later flew Hurricanes with the Merchant Shipping Fighter Unit and No 257 Sqn. This latter unit re-equipped with Typhoons in July 1942, at which point Stapleton became a flight commander. After a 'rest tour' as an instructor at the Central Gunnery School, Stapleton took command of No 247 Sqn, No 124 Wing, in August 1944. From then until 5 December 1944, when it was shot down while being flown by another pilot, Stapleton's Typhoon was MP120/ZY-Y, fondly known as *Excreta Thermo* and decorated with artwork symbolising the destruction of Nazi power by a rocket, painted by Flg Off 'Spy' McKay, the squadron intelligence officer.

Typical of the operations undertaken by the wing in the winter of 1944/45 was one flown on 28 November, described in brief detail in No 247 Sqn's Operations Record Book as follows;

'Six RP Typhoons, led by Sqn Ldr Stapleton DFC, were detailed on Armed Recce of the Rees–Coesfeld–Munster–Wesel area. One loco with 15 trucks at A5151 (12 nautical miles west Haltern) facing south was attacked with RP and cannon. The loco was destroyed and the trucks blew up with a large red flash, followed by a column of smoke. Buildings in the siding were set on fire. One loco facing south at A5155 was damaged and the rail cut, and another loco at A4650 was attacked, with unobserved results. Up at 1110 hrs and down at 1214 hrs.'

The squadron's unofficial diary noted pilots were 'again having to run the dreaded gauntlet of the Reichswald' (a large forest concealing numerous 'flak traps'), and that the attack on the first locomotive – as shown in this specially commissioned cover artwork – had been carried out 'in the face of intense opposition'. Just another routine day for a 2nd TAF Typhoon pilot (*Cover artwork by Mark Postlethwaite*)

First published in Great Britain in 2010 by Osprey Publishing
Midland House, West Way, Botley, Oxford, OX2 0PH
44-02 23rd St, Suite 219, Long Island City, NY 11101, USA

E-mail; info@ospreypublishing.com

ISBN 13: 978 1 84603 973 7
ebook ISBN: 978 1 84603 974 4

Edited by Tony Holmes
Page design by Tony Truscott
Cover Artwork by Mark Postlethwaite
Aircraft Profiles by Chris Thomas
Index by Margaret Vaudrey
Originated by PDQ Digital Media Solutions, Suffolk, UK
Printed and bound in China through Bookbuilders

10 11 12 13 14   10 9 8 7 6 5 4 3 2 1

ACKNOWLEDGEMENTS
Over many years of research into the subject of this book I have received unstinting help and support from Typhoon pilots, groundcrew and their families, and access to their personal archives, for which I am extremely grateful. I hope this publication (which without such assistance would be a somewhat lesser record!) goes some way towards repaying that debt.

CONTENTS

AIRCRAFT AND WEAPONS

The Typhoon had begun life as Hawker Aircraft Limited's successor to its first monoplane fighter, the Hurricane. Although the latter would enjoy great success in combat, serving throughout World War 2 on virtually every front, its airframe was essentially a 'mid-thirties' design. This meant that it was not capable of being significantly developed, and certainly not robust enough to take advantage of the next generation of aero-engines that would follow the Rolls-Royce Merlin.

Hawker duly set about designing an airframe able to harness the power of the Napier Sabre, Rolls-Royce Vulture or Bristol Centaurus engines, all of which promised to deliver in the region of 2000 hp. With the latter delayed, two prototypes were produced – the Vulture-engined aircraft flew first in October 1939, followed by the Sabre-powered variant four months later. When development of the Vulture was terminated, the Sabre-engined machine, now named the Typhoon, became the production type.

The first frontline unit to receive the Typhoon was No 56 Sqn, with examples arriving at its Duxford base in September 1941. Although nominally a frontline fighter squadron, No 56 Sqn effectively became a trials unit for the Typhoon. Indeed, it would be eight months before the first operational sorties were flown. Problems that were obvious from the beginning were that the view to the rear was hopelessly inadequate, the Sabre engine was prone to sudden failure and carbon monoxide was seeping into the cockpit.

Fourth production Typhoon R7579, seen here during evaluation at the A&AEE at Boscombe Down in September 1941, is typical of the early aircraft delivered to No 56 Sqn in the last quarter of 1941. The 'solid' fairing behind the cockpit restricted the rear view so essential for a fighter pilot. A shortage of cannons led to all the early aircraft being delivered as 'Mk IAs', armed with 12 Browning 0.303-in machine guns – the ports for the six closely-grouped guns in the starboard wing can be seen in the leading edge (*A&AEE*)

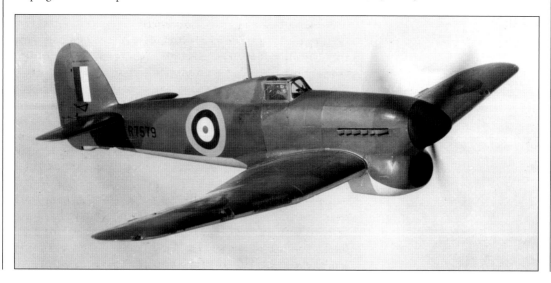

While solutions for these problems were put in hand, aspects of the Typhoon's performance were revealed as less than satisfactory. Although proclaimed as the RAF's first '400 mph fighter', performance fell off rapidly above 15,000 ft, while limited manoeuvrability meant that the Typhoon was never going to be a 'dogfighter'. The latter point should have come as no great surprise to Fighter Command, as the original specification on which the Typhoon tender was based had stated 'a high degree of manoeuvrability is not required'!

Nevertheless, with a new rear canopy, pilots breathing oxygen from start-up to shut-down and engineers working flat out to keep enough Typhoons with serviceable engines available, the aircraft did become operational in mid-1942. Fighter Command (rather reluctantly) tried to integrate the Typhoon-equipped Duxford Wing (Nos 56, 266 and 609 Sqns) with current Spitfire operations, but these efforts were not successful. The wing proved unwieldy when operating at full strength and the Typhoon was not at its best at the altitudes employed by the Spitfire. As a result its operational use came under strict review.

Undeniably, the aircraft had some useful attributes, not least its top speed – in the region of 410 mph at 15,000 ft, but more especially at sea level where its 375 mph made the Typhoon considerably faster than anything else in the sky. The fighter also had an as yet untapped load-carrying potential, a very high cruising speed (290 mph), a considerable range (600 miles) and it was a stable gun platform for its heavy armament of four 20 mm cannons. Finally, the Typhoon proved to be relatively easy to fly at night.

Accordingly, the next squadrons to equip were Hurricane units that had been mainly flying night 'Intruders'. Although some work was done trying to operate the Typhoons with Turbinlite Bostons and Havocs, these squadrons soon joined those of the now disbanded Duxford Wing in being allocated, singly, to airfields along the south and east coasts of England as a measure against German fighter-bombers that were proving difficult to counter. Bomb-carrying Bf 109s and Fw 190s were crossing the Channel and North Sea in a shallow dive down to sea level so as to build up their speed and sneak in below radar cover. Once over land they would make quick 'hit and run' attacks on coastal towns and installations, before fleeing back across the sea to occupied Europe.

Basing the Typhoons along the coast proved to be a fortuitous move, as by the end of 1942 they had claimed 14 German fighters destroyed and two as 'probables'. These successes had not only endorsed Fighter Command's bold plan, they had also restored the Typhoon's previously flagging reputation.

Despite these victories, new problems had arisen, and there was still no solution to the reliability issues surrounding the Sabre engine. Three Typhoons had been shot down by Spitfires and others had been attacked with lethal intent. Coastal anti-aircraft guns were also prone to open up on the new shape in the skies, which from some angles bore an uncomfortable resemblance to the Fw 190. Recognition problems were solved with the introduction of special markings, first in the form of yellow wing bands, then white noses and black underwing stripes and, finally, black and white underwing stripes, which proved most effective. Indeed, they would be worn from January 1942 to February 1944.

However, a most deadly and intractable problem was evident – the growing number of structural failures in the air. The first of these (which almost invariably resulted in the death of the pilot) occurred on 29 July 1942 when a No 257 Sqn Typhoon broke up near High Ercall. The following month a Hawker test pilot was killed when his aircraft fell in pieces among the Staines reservoirs. Just a week later a No 56 Sqn sergeant pilot died when his aircraft plummeted into fields near Spalding. In each case it seemed that the complete tail unit had broken away from the rear fuselage, but what was causing the fracture? Suspicion fell on the rear fuselage joint, and a massive programme of strengthening modifications was carried out.

Between December 1942 and March 1943 more than 300 Typhoons were withdrawn from frontline squadrons and sent to No 13 Maintenance Unit (MU) or the manufacturers for 'Mod 286' – internal and external strengthening of the suspect joint. Most Typhoon pilots then flew on operations blithely believing that the problem was cured. It was, however, anything but, and nine more Typhoons (and eight of their pilots) were lost in the first five months of 1943, bringing the total to 13. Five of the victims were flying 'Mod 286' embodied aircraft. Meanwhile, test pilots at Hawker and the Royal Aircraft Establishment (RAE) had the unenviable job of trying to replicate the failure conditions – fortunately perhaps for them without success.

Although the elevator mass balance had been one of the items under investigation since August 1942, it was not until September 1943 (when a No 183 Sqn Typhoon returned from a dive-bombing sortie, having experienced elevator flutter which damaged the control lever linkages) that the prime cause of the tail failures was isolated. Subsequently, modifications to the elevator mass balance seem to have largely cured the problem, much improving the flying hours per accident rate. Structural failures did still occur, however, and the Typhoon would leave service without a complete remedy to the problem, or indeed a full explanation as to why 26 of them had suffered in flight failures.

FIGHTER-BOMBER

Trials to identify the aircraft type most suited for what was then known as 'Army Support' were carried out by the Air Fighting Development Unit (AFDU) in August 1942. Rather surprisingly, even without the benefit of hindsight, the Mustang I was given the top rating, followed by the Hurricane and Whirlwind, with the Spitfire and Typhoon equal fourth! However, it was decided to take advantage of the Typhoon's low-level performance and firepower by investigating its potential as a fighter-bomber. Accordingly, between 6 and 18 September 1942, the Aircraft and Armament Experimental Establishment (A&AEE) carried out trials on Typhoon R7646, which had been fitted with a single faired bomb rack beneath each wing that was capable of carrying a 500-lb bomb. The results were promising, and providing the fairings were fitted to the racks, there was little effect on handling. Indeed, the aircraft remained steady in the dive up to 400 mph (ASI), although there was increasing buffeting above 350 mph (ASI).

An urgent programme was subsequently initiated to introduce the bomb-carrying modifications on the Typhoon production line.

Displayed for the press at Tangmere on 28 June 1943, DN421/EL-C of No 181 Sqn (based at Tangmere satellite Merston) has a 500-lb bomb slung beneath each wing and wears the underwing identity stripes introduced at the beginning of the year. DN421 was usually flown by Flg Off 'Paddy' King, who was later killed in the first Typhoon rocket attack (*H Collins*)

Meanwhile, Hawker modified Gloster-built aircraft, and the first 'bombers' reached No 181 Sqn in mid-October 1942. Initially, production was split between 'fighter' and 'bomber' versions of the Typhoon, but by the spring of 1943 all aircraft coming off the line were capable of carrying bombs.

Although the type had by now been selected as the main fighter-bomber for the RAF force that would support the forthcoming invasion of occupied Europe, there remained one daunting problem to solve. Despite all this effort to give the RAF a fighter-bomber suitable for combat operations, there remained the millstone of the Typhoon's hopelessly unreliable Sabre engine. In addition, engine production was lagging behind airframe production, resulting in growing numbers of engineless Typhoons in store at MUs and other locations around the country.

The Sabre engine was prone to sudden failure, and this was usually caused by seizure of the sleeve valves. By the end of 1942, engines were routinely removed from Typhoons for inspection after only 25 hours of flying, and the demand for replacement powerplants increased the numbers of engineless airframes in storage. In the spring of 1943 the engine problems were finally solved thanks to the help that Napier received from the Bristol Aeroplane Company, which had much experience of sleeve valves on its radial engines. New materials and techniques were employed in the construction of the Sabre engine that finally brought its serviceability up to acceptable levels.

In May 1943 Air Marshal Sir Trafford Leigh-Mallory, Air Officer Commanding (AOC) Fighter Command, took action to bring some order and efficiency to what had become Typhoon production chaos. With the frontline squadrons absorbing large numbers of new engines, the backlog of engineless Typhoons was not getting any smaller, and some of these airframes were being reduced to components to help the growing demand from repair contractors. It had reached the point were some of the latest aircraft with the fittings for bomb and long-range tank carriage (in short supply on the squadrons) were being dismantled!

Leigh-Mallory called a meeting between Fighter Command, Hawker, Gloster (the main Typhoon producer) and Maintenance Command representatives. In the wake of this gathering, new Typhoons were provided with new engines and delivered to the squadrons, thereby allowing the latter to replace their old machines with up-to-date aircraft with serviceable powerplants. By June 1943 production was running at an average of 24 aircraft per week – more than enough to totally re-equip five squadrons per month. Huge numbers of older machines were withdrawn from service and, in most cases, reduced to components. These parts were needed for use in the repair programmes that were being set up to return the large numbers of damaged machines anticipated during Operation *Overlord* (the Normandy invasion) and the subsequent campaign back to service. By the onset of autumn virtually the entire Typhoon force had been equipped with new aircraft.

At last the Typhoon was 'on the map' – and just in time, as the 18 units equipped with the aircraft were about to become the backbone of the newly formed 2nd Tactical Air Force (TAF). The new Typhoons were all capable of carrying a pair of 250- or 500-lb bombs or two 44-gallon long-range drop tanks, and whilst the squadrons set about developing the tactics to take advantage of these attributes, further developments were in hand.

NEW REFINEMENTS

While serviceability issues were now under control, there were other problems that needed addressing if the Typhoon was to become the ideal ground attack machine. Most pressing were the view from the cockpit, airframe vibration, lack of armour against ground fire and utilising the Typhoon's full potential for weapons carriage and delivery.

Despite the replacement of the early Typhoon canopy fairing with a transparent section, the view from the cockpit was still not good due to the heavy framing. The view to the rear was further impeded by the armoured glass on either side of the head armour and the large aerial mast and its fittings. It was also distorted by the curved rear canopy section. Some improvement was achieved by replacing the aerial mast with an external 'whip' aerial and generally cleaning up the area behind the seat armour. Typhoons with these canopies reached the squadrons from mid-August 1943, although this was only an interim solution as a totally new canopy was on the way. This comprised a new windscreen with much slimmer frames and a sliding hood, with its glazing blown from a single piece of perspex – this would later be known as a 'bubble canopy'.

The latter had been installed on Typhoon R8809 by January 1943, and it received enthusiastic comments from all the pilots that were consulted. However, with the complexity of the changes to the fuselage and the

Hawker test pilot Bill Humble in Typhoon IB R8809, with the trial installation of the sliding 'bubble' hood that revolutionised the view for the pilot. Also on trial on this aircraft are the exhaust fairings that would appear on production Typhoons in August 1943. In practice, the fairings proved more trouble than they were worth, and were discontinued on production aircraft in March 1944 (*Hawker*)

Above and top
An essential element of the programme to keep 20 Typhoon squadrons equipped was the repair and modification of damaged aircraft. This No 1 Sqn Typhoon, JR328/JX-X, was one of the last examples built with the old canopy. Damaged when its brakes failed and the undercarriage collapsed on landing at Martlesham Heath on 6 March 1944, the aircraft was initially repaired by Hawker. Following a visit to Cunliffe-Owen at Eastleigh, JR328 would emerge in a new guise, equipped with RPs and a bubble canopy. It then saw service with No 182 Sqn as XM-D, as seen here at B78 Eindhoven, but was scrapped following damage received in the Luftwaffe's New Year's Day attack, Operation *Bodenplatte* (*S A Lovett via Drs P E van Loo*)

lengthy lead time on components for Gloster's production line, the first production Typhoons with the new canopy did not leave the line until late November 1943 – and even then they were only sporadic examples among the older hooded versions. This situation had been foreseen, and it was also realised that there was insufficient time to wait for the 2nd TAF squadrons to be equipped with the sliding-hood Typhoons if, as desired, the whole force should be so equipped in time for *Overlord*. Accordingly, conversion 'kits' were produced and Gloster, Hawker and contractor Cunliffe-Owen of Eastleigh set about modifying Typhoons still fitted with old canopies that were to be retained in service.

As a ground attack machine it was essential that the Typhoon's vulnerability to ground fire (German flak was lethal) be minimised. Like all aircraft fitted with water-cooled engines, the radiator was particularly vulnerable, especially on the Typhoon with its prominent 'chin' location. Consequently, armour was designed to line the 'radiator bath' (i.e. the fairing that surrounded the vulnerable radiator), as well as the sides and bottom of both the engine compartment and cockpit. Some 780 lbs of armour would be added in total. As with the canopy modifications, it was not possible to make these changes overnight, but once again the modifications were seen as essential for the force that would be providing close support for the forthcoming invasion.

Since its introduction into service, the Typhoon airframe had suffered from a high frequency vibration that was so bad it caused the pilot some considerable discomfort. Touching the side of the cockpit produced a sensation similar to a small electric shock, and rumours abounded that the vibration caused infertility – subsequent events seem to have disproved that one, as the author's father was a Typhoon pilot! Extracts from Sqn Ldr Roland Beamont's report to Fighter Command, having test flown Typhoon R7617 with anti-vibration remedies embodied at Langley at the beginning of January 1943, show that solutions were available;

'This aircraft is fitted with a four bladed constant speed Hydromatic propeller, the engine is mounted on rubber bearers and the pilot's seat has been modified and sprung to lessen vibration. On take-off, full revolutions and boost were used, and there was a complete absence of excess vibration. In addition, the performance of the aircraft with the four-bladed propeller is greatly increased with regard to take-off, initial climb and acceleration.'

The improved engine bearings and sprung seat were quickly introduced, but it would be early 1944 before an attempt was made to usher the four-bladed propeller into service, by which time it had been found that when paired with the larger Tempest tailplane (as trialled on EK229 at the end of 1943), not only were performance and handling improved but vibration and flutter problems were much reduced.

Unfortunately yet another snag lay in wait, however. No sooner had the early production aircraft flown than it was discovered that the oil seals on the propellers were prone to failure, and as a result increasing numbers of new Typhoons were held in 'purgatory store' by Maintenance Command, awaiting resolution. We shall return to this situation later.

ROCKETS!

It was desirable that the Typhoon's full load-carrying capability should be exploited, and a series of trials were carried out to increase the bomb load and, most importantly, to introduce a new weapon – the rocket projectile (RP). The RP, or Unrotating Projectile (UP) as it was originally known, was first used successfully on operations by a Swordfish of No 819 Sqn in May 1943. The following month No 137 Sqn commenced flying Hurricane IVs armed with either 40 mm cannons or RPs. The latter was found to be the more effective weapon, but it could not initially be used

Most of the early RP trials on the Typhoon were carried out by EK497, which, after initial installation and testing by Hawker at Langley in July 1943, went to the A&AEE at Boscombe Down for service trials the following month. In this view EK497 is seen during those latter trials, fitted with Mk IA rails (*A&AEE*)

over occupied territory as it was still considered 'secret'. This restricted the RP's use to anti-shipping missions. Two more Hurricane units – Nos 164 and 184 Sqns – would convert to RPs, and both eventually became part of the 2nd TAF. Meanwhile, trials of the weapon fitted to a Typhoon (EK497) were carried out at A&AEE, and the first RP-equipped aircraft entered service with No 181 Sqn in October 1943 (see Chapter 4).

Early on, Typhoons were fitted with 'Rocket, Projector, Aircraft Mk IAs', which were steel beams with a pair of circular cross-section rails beneath them. They were mounted beneath the wings via a pair of struts that were adjustable to facilitate harmonisation. A set of eight rails weighed 408 lbs, and each rail was wired to the aircraft's electrical circuit and fitted with a socket at the rear, into which plugged the electrical lead (known as a 'pigtail') from the rocket itself.

The rocket motor was a three-inch diameter steel tube filled with propellant. At the rear end were cruciform fins, each 8-in. x 5-in., made from thin steel. The rockets were suspended from the rails by two 'saddles', one near the centre of gravity of the RP and the other just in front of the fins. When first introduced, RPs were fitted with 25-lb armour piercing heads, but in the 2nd TAF the standard warhead was the 60-lb Semi-Armour Piercing/High Explosive (SAP/HE) shell. This had a high explosive charge-to-weight ratio, making it a 'blast' weapon.

In early December 1944 the first 60-lb HE Fragmentation RP heads were delivered, and they were used alongside the SAP/HE rounds until the end of the war. The new heads featured a lower charge/weight ratio (the explosive weighed just four pounds) and had a thicker wall, which gave a good fragmentation effect. This made them particularly deadly against personnel and thin-skinned vehicles.

The only other warhead used operationally on the 2nd TAF RPs was the Bomb 'U' five-inch, which was filled with a phosphorous mixture. It was used for fire-raising or target marking on special operations. Concrete heads could be fitted for practice firings.

A normal RP load for a Typhoon was four under each wing, but they could be used in conjunction with 44-gallon long range tanks (each tank replacing the two inner RP rails) in combinations of two tanks/four RPs or a single tank and six RPs. As a single RP with a 60-lb head weighed in the region of 100 lb, a full load of eight with Mk IA rails totalled over 1200 lb. Trials at A&AEE showed that a Typhoon with this load had its top speed reduced by some 38 mph. This figure was improved by 15 mph with the fitting of lightweight

Armourers of No 6245 Servicing Echelon feed 20 mm cannon shells into the starboard gun bay of MN514/MR-J of No 245 Sqn at B5 airfield in Normandy. Canvas appears to have been doped over the joins in the cannon barrel fairings, probably in an effort to keep out the invasive dust that was causing frequent stoppages. The RP 'beams' are the steel Mk IA type, and the rocket warheads are 60-lb SAP/HE. Note the 'pigtails' – electrical firing leads – hanging at the rear of the rails. After an inadvertent firing incident, it became practice to leave these disconnected until immediately before take-off (*Canadian Forces*)

A close-up of the anti-personnel RP heads, alternating with the more familiar SAP/HE, on a No 175 Sqn Typhoon at the time of the Rhine crossings. The fragmentation heads were tipped with a small propeller that rotated when the RP was fired, eventually extending a rod which detonated the rocket on contact with the ground. The rockets were usually arranged on the rails so that when a pair was fired – i.e. one from each wing – they consisted of one SAP/HE and one fragmentation head (*Canadian Forces*)

(240 lb for eight) aluminium Mk III rails, which were available from December 1944 and soon supplanted the steel rails. It was realised rather late in the day that rails were in fact not required for launching RPs from high-speed aircraft. Subsequently, 'zero-length' launchers were developed during 1945, but they were made available too late to be used in action by Typhoons in Europe.

The firing of RPs was controlled via an auto-selector box and a push button. This enabled the pilot to fire them in pairs (one RP from each wing) or in a salvo. With a deft bit of switch flicking the pilot could also achieve a 'ripple'. Sighting was achieved via the fixed Mk II reflector gunsight, which projected an image directly onto the screen. The Mk II was shown to produce the best results when it came to accurately firing RPs. Some Typhoons were fitted with a sandwich windscreen, however, and this precluded the Mk II's use due to the double image that it projected – these aircraft were fitted with a Mk IIL gunsight instead. In August 1944 a programme to standardise Typhoon windscreens and sights was put in place so as to allow all pilots to use image projection.

READY FOR D-DAY?

So as the end of 1943 approached, 18 of the 20 squadrons required by the Order of Battle for the Allied Expeditionary Air Force (AEAF) were fully equipped with serviceable Typhoons within the 2nd TAF and ADGB (Air Defence of Great Britain, as Fighter Command had been renamed), and two more squadrons were in the process of equipping. However, the 400 or so aircraft assigned to these squadrons were of widely differing modification states. On 17 December 1943, in an effort to develop a viable plan, Leigh-Mallory, now AOC AEAF, analysed the numbers, location and states of the 1756 Typhoons so far delivered as follows;

ADGB and 2nd TAF	412
No 41 Group (Maintenance Command)	56
Under repair	36
Experimental	34
Broken down	701
Purgatory store	289
Lost on operations/accidents	228

The staggering figure of 701 aircraft 'broken down' after, at the most, two years service had arisen from the shortfall of engines for the foreseeable future, and the desire to make *some* use of the redundant airframes. There was little prospect of engines becoming available for the 289 in 'purgatory' either, as all Sabre production was earmarked for the Typhoons coming off the production line and the high priority Tempest which was about to enter service. Further bad news was that of the 412 aircraft in service, only nine had the new sliding hood, although 31 of the aircraft receiving acceptance checks and preparation for service (in No 41 Group) were so equipped.

The figures for aircraft with RP modifications were not listed, but they would have been low. Despite the fact that production aircraft with RP capability were about to arrive at MUs, and production had hit a rate of 100 Typhoons per month, the outlook was still grim. Daily 'wastage' was

Photographed after canopy and RP modifications at Hawker in May 1944, the underside of JR128 displays fresh paintwork, especially where the RP rail connections have been fitted. Note also that the starboard landing light formerly in the wing leading edge has been faired over – a feature of production Typhoons from about this time. Although the aircraft carries the code letters of No 183 Sqn, these relate to its previous service when fitted with the older framed canopy. Shortly after this photograph was taken, JR128 followed the usual route for 2nd TAF Typhoons – to No 51 MU at Lichfield for final acceptance and service fitments, then to a GSU (No 83 in this case). It was flown out to France on 7 August 1944 but lasted just 11 days with No 181 Sqn before it was shot down by flak at Falaise (*Hawker*)

still running at two Typhoons per day, with the prospect of much higher rates to come when *Overlord* started! It was essential, therefore, that the majority of Typhoons in service were modified with all haste. Leigh-Mallory listed the 'mods' required (RP and sliding hood, obviously), but also those necessary for the carriage of bombs and long-range jettisonable tanks, as well as armour protection and other miscellaneous improvements not present on all service Typhoons at that point in time.

After discussions with all concerned, an urgent programme was initiated that would see Typhoons already in service being rotated through Hawker Aircraft, Gloster Aircraft, Cunliffe-Owen or No 13 MU to be brought up to the required standard. Withdrawing the aircraft from service for the programme was itself a problem, as squadron commanders were struggling to retain sufficient Typhoons to meet operational and training demands. More problems were on the way.

As related earlier, the first production aircraft with four-bladed propellers could not be issued due to problems with their oil seals. Suitable replacements were located in the USA, but they were not immediately available. Numbers of airframes held by Maintenance Command steadily rose as a solution was sought. It was possible to fit Typhoons with the large (Tempest) tailplane with a three-bladed propeller, but compensating lead weights had to be added to allay vibration, and this remedy was only effective above 2600 rpm (the Sabre was a high-revving engine, cruising at 3150 rpm, with a maximum of 3700 rpm). Nevertheless, the demand to get these aircraft into use was such that more than 200 Typhoons were fitted with this interim measure.

Further problems came from the use of Cunliffe-Owen as a contractor. This Eastleigh-based company, although having earlier been selected as one of the subcontractors to build the ill-fated Tornado, had no experience with the Hawker type as it had subsequently been occupied with converting Spitfire Vs into Seafires. Progress with the Typhoon modification programme was slow as a result, and it was not until the last weeks of April that an improvement was seen. Nevertheless, as D-Day loomed there were still shortages. Indeed, as late as mid-May No 51 MU (the major unit responsible for final preparation and issuing of Typhoons) at Lichfield was still short of the requisite RP and bomb carrier fittings.

Just to add further pressure to the Typhoon shortage, it was now seen that the supply of adequately trained pilots could not be maintained (and there would no longer be training capacity within the operational units) without converting one of the Hurricane operational training units (OTUs), now named Tactical Exercise Units (TEUs), to Typhoons.

Consequently, No 3 TEU needed 38 Typhoons – it would start work with a pretty motley selection of outdated machines!

After early attempts at switching from bombs to RPs and vice versa when operations demanded either weapon, it was decided to specialise squadrons on one or the other. This would also limit the demand for RP-capable Typhoons. Roughly two-thirds of the Typhoon force would be armed with RPs, No 83 Group fielding two RP wings (Nos 121 and 124) and a single bomber wing (No 143) and No 84 Group one RP wing (No 123) and two mixed bomber/RP wings (Nos 136 and 146). Thanks to the modification programme, all the Typhoon RP squadrons were suitably equipped by D-Day (although a handful of their aircraft still had the old canopy), but it was an extremely close run thing.

NORMANDY CRISIS

Less than a week after D-Day Typhoons were operating from temporary strips carved out of Normandy farmland, and within days the 2nd TAF knew it had a previously unsuspected problem. With the surface vegetation removed by both the Airfield Construction Groups and dry weather, the intensive use of the strips by fighters and fighter-bombers raised ever-increasing clouds of fine dust. Most Spitfires in service were already fitted with Vokes filter systems, while Mustangs were not yet operating from the strips and could therefore be fitted with filters shipped in from the USA. Although three Typhoons had undergone trials in North Africa with what was known as the 'Tropical Air Intake', no decision had been made pre-D-Day to equip the 2nd TAF's aircraft with them. Therefore, it was the Typhoon force that immediately felt the impact of the unavoidable swirling dust.

The problem was recognised as early as 15 June (the fourth day of operations from Normandy strips) when an AEAF engineering officer, having noted aircraft already suffering unserviceabilities due to the

Asymmetric loads – e.g. one bomb and one long-range tank – had been employed when necessary since before D-Day. One of the less common arrangements is seen here on Sgt C J Morgan's No 184 Sqn Typhoon, which carries six RPs and a single 44-gallon long-range tank (*C J Morgan*)

Some idea of the vast dust clouds raised on the Normandy strips can be gained from this shot of XP-A of No 174 Sqn taxiing at B5 Le Fresne-Camilly. The aircraft is almost certainly JP606, which served with that squadron from 27 July to 18 August 1944, when it was damaged by flak (*E Little*)

build-up of silicaceous deposits on the spark plugs, delivered samples of the Calvados dust to the RAE for analysis. He was particularly concerned about the effects the dust would have on the life of the Typhoons' Sabre engines. It was established that more than 80 percent of the dust consisted of hard abrasive material.

Initially, flight tests were undertaken with a simple circular flat deflector plate mounted on the mesh stone-guard fitted to Typhoons at the time, but the problem was becoming more urgent. In three days 17 Typhoons were rendered unserviceable with excessive sleeve wear (the Sabre engine featured sleeve valves which required precise tolerances). It was calculated that an engine would last for only three take-offs! On 19 June all units were ordered to fit a circular plate in front of the air intake as 'first aid'. Back in the UK, while the RAE worked with Vokes to design an installation of a cylindrical air filter, Napier concentrated on developing a modified version of the circular plate that had initially been fitted. The efficiency of the flat plate deflector was tested and calculated to be 53 percent, but Napier's dome deflector proved 88 percent efficient at take-off power. The Vokes/RAE filter system proved even more efficient – 93 percent at take-off power. Although there were pros and cons associated with both systems, they were put into production nevertheless, with 200 of the Napier design ordered and 1500 of the Vokes/RAE version.

With rampant unserviceabilities and shelling at No 124 Wing's B6 and No 121 Wing's intended base, B5 (see Chapter 5), a decision was made to return the Typhoons to their previous airfields at Holmsley South and

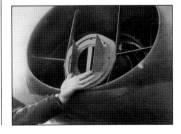

Designed and produced by Napier in a matter of days, the dome dust deflector was the first attempt at a solution to the Calvados dust problem. Only 88 percent efficient, its other major drawback was that an engine backfire would project an extremely hot dome across the airfield, which was not popular with the groundcrews! The dome was soon replaced by a drum filter, designed by Vokes/RAE, that increased efficiency to 93 percent and solved the backfire problem with 'cuckoo doors' that swung outwards with the blast (*via S Coates*)

Hurn. This allowed a massive engineering effort to take place that saw damaged engines (37 on No 121 Wing alone) swapped for new ones and Napier's dome deflectors fitted to all aircraft. The wings returned to B5 and B6 on 27 June once the offending German artillery had been dealt with. The first 300 of the Vokes/RAE filters had been delivered by 2 July, with the remainder supplied by the middle of the month. Once these devices were fitted there were no reported problems with the Typhoons operating in Normandy.

The large number of Vokes/RAE filters ordered reflects this design's adoption as standard for the aircraft

From the autumn of 1944, new production Typhoons were fitted with the Tropical Air Intake, which had been developed from the filters trialled on Typhoons in North Africa. Positioned under the fuselage immediately behind the radiator fairing, the device can be seen here between the inner undercarriage doors in this photograph of late production Typhoon RB452 (*Canadian Forces*)

The oldest Typhoon to see active service in 1945 was R7620 – only the 32nd example of the 3315 production aircraft that were built – which entered service in January 1942 as US-G of No 56 Sqn. It later flew as a propeller development aircraft with de Havilland, before being rebuilt by Taylorcraft in mid-1944. By early 1945 R7620 was in service with No 174 Sqn as XP-P, but on 22 February it was hit in the starboard wing by flak, causing Plt Off Frank Wheeler to crash-land at B80 Volkel. The aircraft narrowly missed No 274 Sqn's Tempest dispersal before it came to a halt inverted (*Frank Wheeler*)

– it became Typhoon Mod 420. However, at the end of June 1944 steps were also taken to introduce the Tropical Air Intake as standard on Typhoons. It was estimated that it would be introduced on the production line towards the end of September, and 1000 sets were to be produced as Mod 421 for retrospective fitting. The author has been unable to establish whether this latter action actually took place, although photographic evidence suggests that the Tropical Air Intakes were introduced on production aircraft in the RB-serial range, which did indeed enter service towards the end of September 1944. In addition, aircraft that were rebuilt from old series or badly damaged airframes also had Mod 421 incorporated. No evidence has come to light to suggest that aircraft were withdrawn from service to fit the Tropical Air Intake, however.

By the autumn of 1944 the Typhoons being delivered were to the ultimate production standard, but the numbers required were only maintained by supplementing new airframes with aircraft rebuilt after damage. Eventually, when sufficient Sabres were finally available, some of those Typhoons that had been lurking in 'purgatory store' for many months were also returned to service as attrition replacements. At one point in early 1944, 200 of these aircraft had been earmarked for conversion into fighter-reconnaissance Typhoon FR IBs, but the programme was terminated in July 1944 after only one squadron was partly equipped, as the aircraft was not really suited to the role, and demand for standard Typhoons remained high. In the last weeks of the war it was possible to see apparently 'new' Typhoons with serials in the R series that had originally been built in 1942!

WEAPONS/STORES DEVELOPMENT

A significant step had been taken in April 1944 by doubling the bombload of the Typhoon. Hawker had conducted initial trials as early as March 1943 on DN340 fitted with two 1000-lb bombs. It proved necessary to move the bomb carrier a few inches outboard so as to take advantage of a stronger position in the wing structure. The performance improvements conferred by the four-blade propeller, especially on take-off, were found to be particularly advantageous when carrying these higher loads. Accordingly, as replacement Typhoons remained a mix of three- and four-bladed aircraft right until the end of the war, bomber units had the priority for the latter.

Retained by Hawker for various trials, DN340 (seen here at the A&AEE at Boscombe Down in September 1943) makes an interesting comparison with DN421 on page 9. DN340 has a four-bladed propeller for trials, but retains the original tailplane. Note that the location of the bomb-carrier (and 1000-lb bomb) is further outboard than for the 500-lb bomb carrier on DN421. This was done so as to take advantage of a better load-bearing structure within the wing (*A&AEE*)

Anti-personnel bombs ('No 23 clusters' with streamlined noses) were cleared for carriage by Typhoons from April 1944, each cluster bomb casing carrying 26 20-lb fragmentation weapons. Problems with the clusters failing to disintegrate and instances of the tail units detaching in flight suggest that the clusters were not very suitable for external carriage by high-speed aircraft.

After trials at Boscombe Down and Porton, M 10 smoke tanks (one of which could be carried under each wing) were used by several of the Typhoon bomber squadrons during exercises with the Army in the spring of 1944. The tanks themselves were somewhat fragile and liable to rust, and as they could not be stored satisfactorily when full this meant that they had to be filled immediately prior to use – the tanks could also be used to deliver chemical weapons. They were not used operationally.

'Bombs, Aircraft, *Nickel* No 2 Mk II' were dropped by Typhoons, particularly during the German retreat from Normandy. *Nickel* was the code name for leaflet operations, and nothing to do with the material used in the construction of the leaflet canister itself. The devices were usually delivered to the squadrons ready-filled with leaflets, although armourers

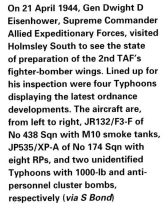

On 21 April 1944, Gen Dwight D Eisenhower, Supreme Commander Allied Expeditionary Forces, visited Holmsley South to see the state of preparation of the 2nd TAF's fighter-bomber wings. Lined up for his inspection were four Typhoons displaying the latest ordnance developments. The aircraft are, from left to right, JR132/F3-F of No 438 Sqn with M10 smoke tanks, JP535/XP-A of No 174 Sqn with eight RPs, and two unidentified Typhoons with 1000-lb and anti-personnel cluster bombs, respectively (*via S Bond*)

The 16-rocket armament load was tested on Typhoon MN861 at the A&AEE at Boscombe Down in August 1944. The rockets were linked pairs, and they remained joined together after firing. The aircraft's handling was found to be unsuitable for operations in this configuration, but there was some limited use made of the paired rockets on the inner pairs of rails only, totalling 12 RPs (*A&AEE*)

were instructed on the filling procedures if required. The canisters were popularly known as 'bumph bombs', and delivering them was not a popular job – just as dangerous as delivering high explosives, but with rather less job satisfaction!

The 2nd TAF was keen to further exploit the Typhoon's load-carrying capability, and one way of delivering more explosives was to use 'double rockets'. These were two standard RPs with 60-lb SAP/HE heads linked together with a No 2 Duplex saddle – one fin was deleted from each RP to facilitate this. The resulting pair could only be fired as a single item, but it was seen as a way of increasing firepower. Trials at the A&AEE had shown that a Typhoon armed with eight of these double RPs was somewhat unwieldy and not suitable for operational use, but if double RPs were loaded on the inner pairs of rails only, then the combination was manageable. A double RP was difficult for armourers to handle, taking about 30 minutes to prepare (as opposed to five minutes for a single RP), and the device was rarely used – only 590 were fired from Mk IA rails.

Later, a different saddle (modified No 2 Duplex) was developed which allowed double RPs to be fitted on the Mk III rails, and a further 381 of

Straddling the outer cannon, an airman guides a No 143 Wing Typhoon out of its dispersal at B100 Goch in April 1945. *Ronnie-Bel-Wayne* is carrying an anti-personnel bomb under the wing, this weapon containing 26 20-lb fragmentation bombs. Although Typhoons had been produced with a landing light in the port wing only since mid-1944, it seems that in 2nd TAF service most of them had this faired over too, as seen here (*Canadian Forces*)

An armourer makes the final adjustments to a 90-gallon napalm-filled drop tank on SW558/DP-V of No 193 Sqn. Note the bomb-carrier braces have been used to offset the tank inboard of the carrier centreline, possibly in an effort to increase ground clearance. This photograph was taken post-war during the summer of 1945, when No 146 Wing Typhoons featured both red spinners and cannon (*C Woodcock*)

After trials with Typhoon RB363 at the Airborne Forces Experimental Establishment at Beaulieu in early 1945, Supply Containers Mk 1 were cleared for carriage and dropping from Typhoons. This facility was used operationally in April 1945 for the dropping of supplies to SAS forces behind German lines (*via A Brown*)

these were fired on operations. A further new saddle (No 4 Duplex) became available shortly before the end of the war that allowed the bottom rockets to be fired independently, but they were too late to see operational use.

A small number of Mk 1 Incendiary bombs were also used on operations by Typhoons. These were 90-gallon ferry tanks filled with napalm that was ignited by an external pistol strapped to the outside of the tank by a steel band. Trials with the standard 44-gallon drop tanks had proven disappointing, and although more effective, the 90-gallon tank was not an ideal choice. The latter was basically a cylinder with a hemispherical nose and conical tail (no fins), and it was immediately unstable when dropped.

Finally, following trials at the Airborne Forces Experimental Establishment at Beaulieu in late 1944, Typhoons were cleared to carry two Mk 1 supply containers. This facility was used by No 146 Wing aircraft to drop supplies to SAS troops operating behind German lines in April 1945.

THE WINGS

'Wings' had been a part of the RAF's organisational structure since the days of the Royal Flying Corps in World War 1, with both flying and non-flying units being identified by sequential numbers. In Fighter Command during World War 2, wings were named after the airfield at which the constituent squadrons were based or, when some squadrons operated from smaller satellite bases, the main fighter station. The wings controlled by the 2nd TAF had a rather different origin, however.

Whilst planning for what would become Operation *Overlord*, senior officers in the RAF recognised that the Army's support air force would need to operate from bases as close to the frontline as possible, and be capable of speedy relocation as it hopefully moved forward! In March 1943 a large-scale exercise involving both Army and RAF units was organised to take place across large areas of southern England.

Known as *Spartan*, the exercise pitted Southland (the Allies) against Eastland (the enemy). The Southland air element had fighter, army support (fighter-bomber), army co-operation (fighter-reconnaissance) and light bomber aircraft. The units in these four categories were organised into a Composite Group ('Z' Group – Eastland had a similar 'X' Group), supported by ancillary units (Group Headquarters, Mobile Operations Room Unit, Airfield Headquarters, Air Stores Parks, Repair

Members of No 181 Sqn shortly after the unit became part of the TAF, but still within Fighter Command. Sqn Ldr Denis Crowley-Milling (later wing commander flying No 121 Airfield) is centre-front with his hands in his pockets. The first three pilots sitting on the wing, from the left, are Flg Off Jimmy Bryant (later to command No 247 Sqn), Flg Off Hugh Collins (shot down and captured on the first Typhoon RP attack) and Plt Off Ted Haddock (No 181 Sqn's first TAF casualty – posted missing on 15 July 1943, but eventually a PoW after a lengthy evasion). Sitting on the right hand 500-lb bomb is Flt Lt 'Jacko' Holmes, who would later command No 197 Sqn and be killed in action leading the unit. Finally, directly beneath the spinner, again with his hands in his pockets, is Flg Off Arthur Vincent, who would become the CO of No 181 Sqn in August 1944 (*H Collins*)

and Salvage Units (RSU), Servicing Commandos, Advanced Landing Ground Signal Sections, Mobile Air Reporting Units, Ground Controlled Interception, Signals and RAF Regiment).

The flying units, other than the light bomber squadrons, were to operate from 'mobile airfields', and these units were numbered as Nos 121, 122, 123 and 124 Airfields. They did not have squadrons permanently allocated – they were to be used on what was described at the time as a 'hotel and garage basis'.

For *Spartan* only the first two of these Airfields were actually moved to different locations during the 12-day exercise.

The exercise was deemed to be so successful that the organisation of 'Z' Group and its units was retained to form the basis of what would become No 83 Group on 1 April 1943. Exactly two months later the Tactical Air Force (TAF) was formed within Fighter Command, taking in No 83 Group with its four Airfields, each of which was administered by a headquarters unit and occupied by Typhoon, Spitfire or Mustang squadrons. No 2 Group, with its light and medium bomber units, was also transferred to TAF control from Bomber Command. The following month a second composite group was formed – No 84 – which took over No 123 Airfield HQ and formed further new Airfield HQs. Meanwhile, Army Co-operation Command was disbanded and all of its Mustang I squadrons were transferred to Fighter Command, many being allocated to the new TAF.

At this point, the first units entitled 'wings' were formed within the TAF. Initially, they were numbered Nos 15, 16, and 17 Wings, and each of these controlled two of the Airfield HQs. As each of the Airfields had two or (more usually) three squadrons – the equivalent of a normal RAF fighter wing – this seems a bit odd, but it was considered that in the forthcoming invasion of northwest Europe the Airfield HQs would be too mobile for effective administration. Each of the wings was commanded by a group captain and the Airfields by a wing commander, with a further wing commander to look after operations. The latter post was initially known as wing commander flying, later wing commander operations, and colloquially as 'wing leader'.

At first there was much swapping of squadrons between the Airfields, but by the time the TAF was formally promulgated as an independent force on 15 November 1943, and renamed as the 2nd Tactical Air Force (2nd TAF), the No 83 Group Typhoon squadrons were established at Nos 121 an 124 Airfields. The first Typhoon squadron was transferred to No 84 Group nine days later, and it would be joined by many more in the new year. The allocation of Typhoon squadrons to the 2nd TAF Airfields and wings is detailed in full in Appendix 1.

The first few months of 1944 were an extremely busy time for the Typhoon wings. Three new units had been formed by the re-equipment

Wg Cdr 'Reg' Baker (third from the left), wing commander flying Harrowbeer, is seen here with pilots of Nos 193 and 266 Sqns after a successful attack on Etampes-Mondesir airfield on 10 February 1944. Over the following two months both squadrons and Baker would make a series of moves that brought them together at No 146 Airfield, Needs Oar Point. To the right of Baker is Flt Lt John Deall of No 266 Sqn, which he would later command, before going on to become 'Wingco Ops' No 146 Wing in 1945 (*Helen Crassweller*)

of Hurricane IV squadrons, and two of these would immediately be allocated to the 2nd TAF. Three Royal Canadian Air Force (RCAF) units arrived from Canada and began their work-ups on Typhoons, while the remaining Fighter Command Typhoon squadrons, bar Nos 137 and 263 Sqns, were allocated to the new force. These two units were retained in Fighter Command to operate the 'Channel Stop' strategy from Manston and Harrowbeer, respectively. Both squadrons would later join the 2nd TAF in Normandy.

More changes took place as units prepared for their new roles in the 2nd TAF. During January No 174 Sqn had been the first of the Typhoon units to attend the Armament Practice Camp (APC) at Eastchurch to hone its skills with the new rocket-firing equipment. In March and April nearly all remaining units would attend APCs at Eastchurch, Llanbedr or Hutton Cranswick, in rotation, training in either the rocket launching role or as fighter-bombers. Experience had shown that constant practice was necessary to maintain efficiency in either of these arts, and that the man-hours required to change Typhoons from bomber to rocket-firing configuration and vice-versa was prohibitive. Therefore, each squadron was to specialise from now on. Accordingly, Nos 174, 175, 181, 182, 184, 245 and 247 Sqns in No 83 Group and Nos 164, 183, 198 and 609 Sqns in No 84 Group were to operate with rockets. The remainder would fly as bombers.

There was also a flurry of squadron movements (see Appendix 1) between Airfields, notably in No 84 Group, whose newly joined

No 146 Wing operated two Typhoon FR IBs (the fighter-reconnaissance version of the aircraft) to record the results of its attacks. EK372/B, armed with just two cannon, had the port inner gun position occupied by a forward-facing camera – a local modification designed by Flt Lt David Ince. This was found to be effective for photographing heavily defended targets (*D H G Ince*)

Fully armed and ready for take-off, MN666/CG of No 121 Wing is seen at Holmsley South on or shortly after D-Day, with wing commander flying, Charles Green, in the cockpit. Green used it to lead the first RP attack at H+20 on the morning of 6 June 1944 (*N Wilson*)

For a short period at the beginning of July 1944 all the No 20 Sector Typhoon wings were based at Hurn. This historic photograph was taken some time between 3 and 12 July, when only one squadron was missing (No 266 Sqn was at APC Eastchurch) from Nos 123, 136 and 146 Wings. It includes the pilots and squadron officers of Nos, 164, 183, 193, 197, 198, 257 and 609 Sqns. The second row contains the squadron and wing commanders, and they are, starting third from the left, Sqn Ldrs P H Beake (CO No 164 Sqn), J C Button (CO No 193 Sqn), D M Taylor (CO No 197 Sqn), Wg Cdr W Dring (No 136 Wing), Wg Cdr J R Baldwin (No 146 Wing), unknown, Grp Capt D E Gillam (No 20 Sector), unknown, Wg Cdr R E P Brooker (No 123 Wing) and Sqn Ldrs W C Ahrens (CO No 257 Sqn), Y P E H Ezanno (CO No 198 Sqn), L E J M Geerts (CO No 609 Sqn) and The Honourable F H Scarlett (CO No 183 Sqn) (*P G Murton*)

Typhoon squadrons had not experienced the joys of 'mobility' and life under canvas to the same extent as their No 83 Group colleagues. As the better weather approached, the Airfields moved to their *Overlord* bases, under canvas on ALGs or as extra residents on more permanent stations. No 146 Airfield moved to a new ALG at Needs Oar Point, near Beaulieu, while Nos 123 and 136 Airfields settled at Thorney Island. All of these came under the control of No 20 Wing.

At this time the squadrons were also split up for service on the Continent. While the air parties, with small administration sections, retained the unit number, the ground staff were organised as separately numbered Servicing Echelons (by adding a '6' prefix to the squadron number). The intention was that during the invasion, and any advances which followed, the echelons could move from airfield to airfield at short notice, servicing any air party that happened to arrive. While a convenient and sensible arrangement in theory, it had the less fortunate aspect of separating the faithful groundcrews from 'their' squadron. In the event, however, servicing echelons were to remain closely linked with their original squadrons throughout the rest of the war.

On 12 May came a change that brought more logical identities to the units in the 2nd TAF. The previous wings, which in effect were concerned with planning and control, were renamed sectors and the airfields received the more appropriate wing designation. The final changes, which would see the new wings in the formation that would take them through the campaign in northwest Europe, took place at the end of July. Experience had shown the sectors to be unwieldy in operation and they were disbanded. The wings, now with group captains commanding, reported directly to their parent group. No 136 Wing was disbanded, its squadrons joining No 123 Wing, so No 84 Group now had two four-squadron wings.

In August the last two ADGB Typhoon units – Nos 137 and 263 Sqns, which had at last been relieved of their 'Channel-stop' role – joined Nos 124 and 146 Wings, respectively. The progress of the wings from France to Germany can be traced in the tables in Appendix 1.

THE LEADERS

Much of the success of the Typhoon wings in action can be put down to the leadership of sections, flights, squadrons and, most especially, the wings. By the time the invasion was imminent, the tortuous development of the Typhoon both technically and operationally had in turn developed a pool of experienced pilots with the motivation and skills to fill those demanding roles.

Pre-eminent among those men was Denys Gillam, who finished his RAF service career with the Distinguished Service Order (DSO) and two bars, Distinguished Flying Cross (DFC) and bar and an Air Force Cross (AFC), making him one of the most highly decorated fighter pilots. Born in Tynemouth in 1915, Gillam had joined the RAF in 1935, and following service with Hawker Demon-equipped No 29 Sqn, he was posted to the Meteorological Flight at Aldergrove. Gillam was awarded his AFC for twice delivering food from Aldergrove to Rathlin Island in a Westland Wallace after the latter had been cut off from supplies by gales in March 1938.

Upon the outbreak of war he was transferred to No 616 Sqn, and flew Spitfires for a year, claiming six aircraft destroyed, three probables and three damaged in the Battle of Britain. In September 1940 Gillam was posted as flight commander to new Hurricane unit No 312 (Czech) Sqn. At the end of November he was given command of No 306 (Polish) Sqn upon its formation. After an uneventful winter flying night sorties and a spell as a staff officer at No 9 Group HQ, Gillam was back in the frontline again as CO of Hurricane-equipped No 615 Sqn in July 1941. He survived an action-packed two months at Manston operating as part of the 'Channel Stop' campaign that was designed to deny the use of the English Channel to German shipping.

It was here that Gillam honed his low-flying and attack skills in an extremely tough environment, taking on various small motor vessels, armed trawlers, E-boats and flak ships with cannon- or machine gun- (and occasionally bomb-) armed Hurricanes, and sometimes having to engage escorting Bf 109s. Clips of combat film showing Gillam's low-level attacks would be used to show trainee (and operational!) fighter-bomber pilots just how it should be done. In several months No 615 Sqn lost eight pilots killed or captured, with a handful of others wounded. One of the latter was Gillam himself, who was forced to bail out into the Channel on 23 November. This

Grp Capt Denys Gillam briefs No 197 Sqn pilots on their next operation while at B51 Lille/Vendeville (*No 197 Sqn records*)

On 3 October 1944 His Majesty King George VI visited No 146 Wing at B70 Deurne. Here, Grp Capt Denys Gillam is presented to the King by the AOC No 84 Group, Air Vice-Marshal L O Brown (*No 146 Wing records*)

short but eventful tour brought Gillam a DSO, and enhanced his reputation for hard-nosed, uncompromising leadership from the front.

When he returned from a lecture tour in the USA in March 1943, he was perhaps the natural choice for the post of wing commander flying, Duxford, just as the third squadron of what would be the first Typhoon wing arrived to exchange its Spitfires for problem-plagued Typhoons. It was a difficult time as the Duxford Wing struggled to integrate its Typhoons with Fighter Command's established Spitfire operations and it was not long before the wing was disbanded.

Following a three-month course at Staff College and a spell at No 12 Group HQ, Gillam was back flying as commanding officer of the Specialised Low Attack Instructors' School (SLAIS) at Milfield. The first course of students consisted entirely of wing and squadron commanders, many of whom would take up roles in the new TAF being formed in Fighter Command. During this appointment, as in all his non-operational jobs, Gillam would 'sneak off' to keep his hand in, flying unofficial operational sorties with his old squadrons. In July 1943 he was himself posted to the new TAF, first to form and command No 121 Airfield and then to act as its wing commander flying. This posting was short-lived, as in August he attended further staff training in the USA, returning in November to replace Des Scott as Tangmere Wing leader, with Nos 197 and 486 Sqns under his control.

By now Gillam had acquired a reputation as a difficult man to follow, with his 'No 2s' having to be selected from the most experienced pilots, rather than 'new boys' gaining experience. New Zealander Allan Smith, then a flight commander with No 486 Sqn RNZAF who was approaching the end of an 18-month tour on Typhoons and who would later lead No 197 Sqn in Gillam's Wing, once volunteered to fill the hot 'No 2' slot himself;

'I was soon to know why all the other "No 2s" remembered their flights with him. I needed all my flying skill and experience to stay with him. He was like quicksilver – I don't think he, or anybody in the air with him, knew what he was going to do next. He was an aggressive pilot who made a very determined attack on every target.'

With the expansion of the 2nd TAF, Gillam became wing commander flying No 146 Airfield in February 1944, but the following month he was promoted to group captain, OC No 20 (Fighter) Wing. Nevertheless, he continued to fly on operations – no less than three on D-Day. In July 1944, with the reorganisation and renaming of Sectors and Airfields, he became OC No 146 Wing. By August the wing had five squadrons, and it was unique in that they were equipped with bombs and rockets – other wings specialised in one weapon or the other. This enabled Gillam to mastermind some of the great set piece attacks of the war (see Chapter 5). Eventually, at the end of February 1945, he was posted to No 84

Group HQ as group captain operations, and even in this post he slipped away to fly seven more sorties before the war ended.

Inevitably, Gillam had lost a lot of 'No 2s' – allegedly 13 in all – and eventually some cynical wag amended his nickname from 'Killer' to 'Kill 'em' Gillam. He drove himself hard and expected his pilots to follow suit – most did. He did not suffer fools or indiscipline gladly. Just after D-Day, Gillam lost one of his wing commanders who had failed to jettison his long-range tanks before attacking and was shot down in flames by flak. His loss prompted Gillam to grimly remark, 'Men who disobey orders can expect to be killed'. Such was the man who set the pace for the 2nd TAF's Typhoon wings.

Among Gillam's squadron commanders when he led the Duxford Wing was Charles Green, a tough Southern Rhodesian who would become another driving force in the 2nd TAF's Typhoon wings. Green had begun his war flying Coastal Command Ansons, progressing to Blenheim fighters before a posting to No 266 'Southern Rhodesia' Sqn introduced him to Spitfires. In October 1941 Green was promoted to command this unit, which three months later became the second Typhoon squadron. At the end of his first successful tour Green became chief flying instructor at No 59 OTU, returning to operations in January 1944 as wing commander flying No 121 Airfield.

When the wing was under fire at B5 in Normandy it was Green who personally led the attacks to neutralise the offending German artillery. It was also Green who spotted the German armour poised to split the Allied lines at Mortain, and who organised his wing to smash the counter-attack. In the confusion of Falaise he had been despatched by Air Vice Marshal Harry Broadhurst to establish the identity of the columns of vehicles heading east. He returned to advise Broadhurst that he had flown over the columns at 50 ft, and they were German. 'Are you sure?' said Broadhurst, to which Green unequivocally replied 'I saw their black crosses and the square heads of the drivers'!

Promoted again shortly after this episode and given command of No 124 Wing, he continued to fly on operations whenever he saw the chance, mostly logging the sorties as 'local flying'. Green was awarded a DSO to add to the one he already wore, alongside two DFCs. On Boxing Day 1944 flak finally caught up with the combative Rhodesian during an unofficial 'weather recce', and he was forced to bail out into captivity.

The two other Duxford squadron commanders, No 609 Sqn's Paul Richey and No 56 Sqn's 'Cocky' Dundas, both got overseas postings away from the Typhoon, but there were others establishing reputations that would take them to the forefront of operations with the Hawker fighter. Before he was posted to the Mediterranean theatre Dundas was promoted to wing commander to lead the new Typhoon wing that was forming at Duxford in the autumn of 1942.

The new wing was to be equipped with the fighter-bomber, which was only just becoming available, and the two newly-formed squadrons had a long wait to receive their full complement of aircraft. One of the new units, No 181 Sqn, was led by Denis Crowley-Milling, who had been operational with No 615 Sqn in the Battle of France and with Douglas Bader's No 242 Sqn throughout the Battle of Britain. As a flight commander in No 610 Sqn, he was shot down over France on 21 August 1941 but evaded capture,

Charles Green, seen here as a squadron leader with No 266 Sqn, went on to lead No 121 Wing and then command No 124 Wing prior to being shot down and captured on a 'weather reconnaissance' on 26 December 1944 (*C Green*)

escaping with the help of the resistance to Spain, where he was interned for three months before returning to the UK. Posted to form No 181 Sqn in September 1942, Crowley-Milling would eventually lead the unit on some of the first squadron-strength Typhoon bomber operations. After Exercise *Spartan*, his squadron operated with No 124 Airfield in the newly formed No 83 Group.

Following some 11 months in command of No 181 Sqn, 'Crow' moved across to the 'sister' Airfield, No 121, as wing commander flying, but in October 1943 his wartime operational flying came to an end with postings first as a liaison officer with the USAAF and then to Operational Requirements. Post-war, Crowley-Milling would command Tempest, Vampire and Meteor units, before proceeding through varied staff posts and eventually retiring as an air marshal.

No 56 SQN 'OLD BOYS'

Perhaps not surprisingly, the first Typhoon unit, No 56 Sqn, was a breeding ground for future leaders. Among the personnel posted in during 1942 were two Norwegian Spitfire pilots, Erik Haabjorn and Gunnar Piltingsrud. Whilst Piltingsrud became a flight commander with No 56 Sqn and was later killed whilst leading No 137 Sqn, Haabjorn, having survived a dunking in the North Sea after being shot down in error by a Spitfire, was eventually posted to No 609 Sqn as a flight commander. He duly became CO of No 247 Sqn in August 1943. Five months later Haabjorn replaced Derek Walker as wing commander flying No 124 Airfield when the latter was posted to 2nd TAF HQ. Haabjorn led the Airfield/Wing through the rest of the *Noball* anti V-weapon campaign, the vicious anti-radar attacks and the Normandy invasion until the end of August 1944, when he took a staff appointment at the Fighter Leaders' School.

During May 1944 Haabjorn twice more bailed out at low-level into the sea. Sqn Ldr Robin McNair, commanding officer of No 247 Sqn, former Hurricane Battle of Britain and nightfighter pilot and No 245 Sqn flight commander, had witnessed both incidents (the first taking place on the 9th);

'About 40 miiles from the Kent coast Erik gave his call-sign and said "My engine's stopping". The next thing I saw was Typhoon "EH" zooming up from sea level with a dead propeller. At 500 ft or so, when the aircraft was nearly stalling, Erik jumped out both quickly and cleanly, and almost at once his parachute began to stream and open. The whole thing was an amazingly deft performance.'

Wg Cdr Erik Haabjorn (centre) with his engine and airframe fitters in Normandy at the end of his operational flying. Posted to the Central Fighter Establishment as wing commander tactics, he toured the 2nd TAF wings in an Anson in order to keep abreast of developing tactics. The Anson was destroyed during the Luftwaffe's New Year's Day attack on B78 Eindhoven, but Haabjorn took revenge on a Fw 190 with a bren gun! (*Jack Snape*)

Haabjorn was picked up safely, but just 13 days later it was a somewhat closer call;

'We attacked a radar station just north of Dieppe with cannons and rockets, and Erik went in first from a landward direction, leading Nos 181 and 182 Sqns, and I came in second with No 247 Sqn. He flew very low so as to be sure of hitting the target, and I feared that he might be hit by debris from the buildings, but he was struck by flak as we headed out over the coast, just north of the harbour. His engine was trailing smoke and he was still flying very low. Just after he had passed the outer harbour wall his engine stopped. Erik pulled hard on the stick, came up to about 700 ft and leapt out in his practised manner! Soon he was in his dinghy, but in clear sight of the harbour wall – he told me afterwards that he could see a German sentry pacing up and down. Since Erik was so close to the shore, and in danger of being picked up by an enemy vessel, or shot up by an aircraft, a protective beehive of Typhoons gathered over him. Erik was soon back at Hurn.

'To one who had escaped from Norway across the North Sea in an open boat, a few hours in a rubber dinghy was small trouble. He was a brave and fine leader, and all this was good for morale.'

During this period, No 123 Wing was commanded by ace Wg Cdr Peter Brooker. He had a lengthy fighter pilot's pedigree, having flown Hurricanes with No 56 Sqn before the war and through the Battle of Britain, commanding No 1 Sqn in 1941 and No 232 Sqn in Singapore. Taking the No 123 Wing leader post in May 1944, he too experienced immersion in the Channel after being hit by flak whilst attacking a radar, and when picked up some 25 miles south of Beachy Head, he seemed more perturbed to find that his watch was not waterproof as advertised than by his predicament! Brooker later led No 122 Wing (Tempests) but failed to return from a sortie on 16 April 1945. Almost certainly shot down by Fw 190s, Brooker's crash site was never found.

Two other No 56 Sqn 'old boys' also commanded Typhoon wings. William Dring (from a Lincolnshire farming family, he was inevitably known as 'Farmer') went on to command No 183 Sqn and took over the lead of No 136 Wing when Wg Cdr Bryan was killed. At the end of July 1944 the wings were reorganised and, with No 136 disbanded, Dring moved over to No 123 Wing, allowing Wg Cdr Brooker to be rested. Perhaps the wing's greatest moment came when all four squadrons combined to halt a determined German counter-attack aimed at reopening the closed jaws of the Falaise pocket. This was an urgent and difficult operation (Canadian, Polish and German forces were occupying a confined area), but a good briefing, co-operation with Visual Control Posts (VCP) and Dring's leadership brought a

At the beginning of December 1944 the Supreme Commander, Allied Expeditionary Force, General Dwight D Eisenhower visited No 123 Wing at B77 Gilze-Rijen. 'Ike' is seen here getting a briefing on RP equipment from Grp Capt Desmond Scott, while Wg Cdr 'Farmer' Dring looks on (*D J Scott*)

successful result, and a DSO for 'Farmer' to add to the DFC he had earned in earlier service. It was a shock to all his comrades when he was killed returning from a weather test during the Ardennes campaign, his Typhoon skidding off an icy runway and turning over.

Yet another No 56 Sqn flight commander spent the rest of the war flying Typhoons, Mike Ingle-Finch going on to command No 175 Sqn from the autumn of 1943 through to the following autumn. After a rest from frontline flying, he returned as wing commander operations (the term wing commander flying seems to have been replaced by wing commander operations about the time the Airfields were renamed as wings) with No 124 Wing in May 1945, replacing Wg Cdr Webb who had been killed just 48 hours prior to the German surrender.

Like No 56 Sqn, No 609 Sqn produced more than its share of leaders. Wg Cdr Alec Ingle had flown with No 605 Sqn in the Battle of Britain and, after a spell as an instructor at an OTU for which he received an AFC, led No 609 Sqn, developing tactics for anti-shipping Typhoon operations. Awarded a DFC for this latter work in August 1943, Ingle was promoted to fill the No 124 Airfield post, but he was shot down by Fw 190s of JG 26 whilst attacking Beauvais-Tille airfield on 11 September and captured.

Ingle's next but one successor as commanding officer of the famous auxiliary squadron, Johnny Wells, also went on to command a wing. Having completed his first operational tour between May 1942 and June 1943, Wells spent six months as a Napier test pilot before rejoining No 609 Sqn. He was almost immediately promoted to command the

Some weeks after the news that German Supreme Commander in the West, General Feldmarschall Erwin Rommel, had died after his staff car had been strafed on 17 July 1944, initial investigations had indicated that the attack had been carried out by pilots from No 193 Sqn, led by Wg Cdr 'Johnny' Baldwin. The men responsible were gathered for publicity photographs – Baldwin is centre right, hand on the map. Rommel's demise was later credited to No 602 Sqn, however (*courtesy Associated Newspapers*)

unit, which enjoyed a very successful period under his leadership. Having seen No 609 Sqn through the invasion of France, Wells went on rest again before returning to operations in November 1944 as a replacement for tour-expired Johnny Baldwin in No 146 Wing. When Grp Capt Gillam's long tour of duty came to an end in February 1945 it was Wells who took his place as commanding officer.

Wells' 'Wingco Ops' slot was taken by another veteran Typhoon pilot, although this time not from No 609 Sqn. Southern Rhodesian Johnny Deall had served with Duxford's other Typhoon unit, No 266 Sqn. Having worked his way up from pilot officer to flight commander during his first tour, Deall was rested in the summer of 1944 before returning to operations with No 193 Sqn in September of that year. He was soon transferred back to No 266 Sqn as its CO after his old comrade Sqn Ldr 'Barney' Wright became a PoW. Post-war, Deall eventually became Deputy Chief of Air Staff in the Southern Rhodesian Air Force.

Pilot officer to group captain in less than three years was impressive progress, but the man whose place Johnny Wells had taken at the head of No 146 Wing, Johnny Baldwin, had progressed even faster. Joining No 609 Sqn in November 1942, Baldwin had become the first Typhoon ace in August 1943 and then gone on to command No 198 Sqn during its very successful long-range intruding spell in the winter of 1943/44. Rested in March 1944, he was brought back to operations in mid-June and given the difficult task of filling Wg Cdr Reg Baker's shoes (see below).

Baldwin proved a very successful wing leader, while his air combat score rose to 15.5 confirmed – the highest for a Typhoon pilot. Flying at least 110 operations (perhaps as many as 170) in just four months, Baldwin was first grounded and then sent on rest as wing commander planning at No 84 Group Control Centre. However, only four months later he was back, now as a group captain, to replace Desmond Scott at the head of No 123 Wing – both his old units, Nos 198 and 609 Sqns, were under his command. As a group captain, he was not officially allowed to fly on operations, but he managed another 16 before the ceasefire. Baldwin had been awarded two DSOs and two DFCs by then. A more

In March 1945, when commanding No 123 Wing, Grp Capt J R Baldwin had two Typhoons for his personal use – one rocket-equipped and one bomber aircraft. The latter, SW496/JB, is seen here. Baldwin was the top-scoring Typhoon pilot in air combat, and the starboard side of this machine was marked with his scoreboard (*J R Baldwin*)

detailed history of this outstanding officer can be found in *Osprey Aircraft of the Aces 27 – Typhoon and Tempest Aces of World War 2*.

During Baldwin's time leading No 123 Wing, his wing commander operations was 'Zipp' Button, who had earlier completed a Typhoon tour as commanding officer of No 193 Sqn in No 146 Wing when Baldwin was wing commander operations. The two worked well together, having flown these sorts of operations whilst serving with No 146 Wing. Button usually flew his black and white decorated Typhoon, which had one cannon replaced by a forward-facing camera and a cine camera in the starboard landing light bay, which he routinely used to record attacks for later analysis.

WHIRLWIND PILOTS

Two Typhoon wing leaders boasted previous time on Westland Whirlwinds, although they came from very different RAF backgrounds.

E R 'Reg' Baker had joined the air force before the war, qualifying as a flying boat pilot and being credited with the destruction of three U-boats whilst serving with Sunderland-equipped No 210 Sqn. In mid-1942, exhausted after a long tour of operations, he crashed his aircraft and was grounded for five months. Baker eventually returned to flying duties via a fighter OTU course! Posted to fly Typhoons with No 182 Sqn, he survived a crash near Ford after being hit by flak attacking Abbeville in May 1943, and a month later he was posted to lead Fighter Command's only remaining Whirlwind unit, No 263 Sqn (the other, No 137 Sqn, was then in the process of re-equipping with Hurricane IVs).

A tough six months followed with anti-shipping sorties – including bombing the priority target *Munsterland* (a blockade-runner with a cargo of Wolfram) three times in Cherbourg harbour – and attacks on communications installations in Normandy and Brittany. At the end of the year Baker was rewarded with a bar to his DFC and promotion to wing commander flying, Harrowbeer. In March he transferred to Tangmere to hold the same position with No 146 Airfield, where his two Harrowbeer units, Nos 193 and 266 Sqns, would join the resident Nos 197 and 257 Sqns. Leading his wing to a new base at Needs Oar Point, south of Beaulieu, in April, Baker proved to be a popular and charismatic leader prior to being killed in action on 16 June 1944 when his Typhoon fell to flak. A DSO was later announced, dated for the day before he died.

Mike Bryan was one of No 137 Sqn's early Whirlwind pilots, having joined the unit in November 1941 as a pilot officer. He soon proved himself to be both competent and aggressive, sharing in the destruction of a Do 217 and claiming an Fw 190 'probable'. Bryan also built up an impressive score of trains damaged or destroyed. He took over 'A' Flight in February 1943, and the following month received a DFC for his air combat claims and his success on 'Intruder' missions – his train tally by then stood at 20 destroyed. By August of the same year this figure had risen to 35 trains, and he had also sunk a number of enemy surface vessels.

Awarded a bar to his DFC, Bryan took command of Typhoon-equipped No 198 Sqn at month-end and undertook similar operations to those in which No 137 Sqn had been engaged, plus sweeps over occupied France and the Low Countries. During these operations he claimed one and one shared

Fw 190s destroyed. Handing over No 198 Sqn to Johnny Baldwin in November 1943, he took a staff appointment but was still able to undertake occasional operations with his old unit. During one of these, in January 1944, he claimed a twin-engined aircraft over Poix and shared in the destruction of a Bf 109. Bryan returned to No 198 Sqn in April 1944 when Baldwin went on rest, but he was soon promoted to wing commander and placed in charge of newly formed No 136 Wing. On 10 June his aircraft was hit by flak while leading No 183 Sqn in an attack on an enemy column south of Caen. Unfortunately, Bryan had failed to release his drop-tanks before commencing his attack run, and these caught fire. He was killed when his Typhoon crashed north of Falaise.

Among the wing leaders were several pilots that had served overseas prior to joining the Typhoon force. Derek Walker, mentioned earlier, had been a Blenheim bomber pilot before switching to Hurricanes in the Middle East and then returning to the UK as an instructor at a Hurricane OTU. 'Billy' Drake, however, had flown fighters since the Battle of France, notably in the Middle East, and he had amassed a score of more than 20 victories (the majority while flying Kittyhawks). Leading No 136 Wing from its early days with one Typhoon and one Hurricane squadron, his career path changed in April 1944 after a disagreement with the newly promoted Grp Capt Denys Gillam – the latter had him posted to the Fighter Leaders' School (FLS).

Another Kittyhawk pilot from the Middle East, Mike Judd, with little experience of Typhoons, was brought in as a replacement for the Canadian Wing's leader, Wg Cdr 'Bob' Davidson, when he went missing in May 1944. Judd successfully led the Canadians throughout the Normandy campaign, but moved across to No 121 Wing in October 1944. His replacement was Frank Grant, previously CO of No 438 Sqn RCAF, who had earlier flown Kittyhawks in the Aleutians and Spitfires with No 504 Sqn. Grant continued in his post until the wing disbanded after the war.

Bill Pitt-Brown flew Mohawks in India until he returned to the UK to serve as an instructor at SLAIS, prior to taking command of No 174 Sqn in February 1944. Promoted to lead No 121 Wing in August 1944 when already in the latter stages of his Typhoon tour, 'PB', as he was usually known, was replaced by Mike Judd after a difference of opinion with Air Vice Marshal Harry Broadhurst.

When Mike Judd completed his spell with No 121 Wing in February 1945, his replacement was Jimmy Keep, an ex-flying instructor, Defiant nightfighter and catapult-Hurricane pilot. After a course at SLAIS and three months with No 182 Sqn, he took command

Wg Cdr R T P 'Bob' Davidson is seen in the cockpit of JP496/R-D whilst leading No 121 Airfield in the autumn of 1943. He transferred to No 143 Wing RCAF soon after it was formed, but was forced to land in France on 8 May 1944. Evading German search parties, Davidson fought with the Maquis until meeting up with the liberating forces. His unusual scoreboard shows victories over two Japanese, two Italian and a single German opponent – another swastika was added before he went missing (*Canadian Forces*)

A regular Army officer, 'Kit' North-Lewis transferred to Army Co-operation Command to fly Blenheim IVs and Mustang Is, before converting to Typhoons early in 1944. By August of that year, North-Lewis was 'Wingco Ops' No 124 Wing – a position he held until just after the Rhine crossings, by which time he had flown 175 operational missions on Typhoons alone (*C D North-Lewis*)

of No 181 Sqn in November 1943. Keep's tour was cut short when his aircraft was hit by flak during an attack on Cherbourg radar station, and he was forced to ditch just ten miles from the target. With bad facial injuries, including a broken jaw, Keep was rescued by a Walrus crew who were then unable to take off in the rough seas. The injured pilot was transferred to a launch for the trip home. It was eight months before Keep flew again, when he logged just 30 minutes in a Miles Master and two hours in Typhoons prior to joining No 121 Wing as its 'wingco' operations!

'Kit' North-Lewis was a regular Army officer who volunteered for flying duties and was transferred to Army Co-operation Command. After flying Blenheims in No 13 Sqn (and taking part in the first 1000-bomber raid on Germany), he converted to the tactical reconnaissance Mustang I and was operational on this type from August 1942 to January 1944, winning the DFC. In January 1944 the squadron that North-Lewis had been due to take over was disbanded, so he volunteered to join the Typhoon force. Initially, he was posted to No 175 Sqn, but at the end of February he transferred to No 182 Sqn as a flight commander.

When 'Jimmy' Keep was shot down and injured on 23 May 1944, North-Lewis moved across the airfield at Hurn to take command of No 181 Sqn. He led this unit through the Normandy campaign until Erik Haabjorn completed his operational tour, at which point North-Lewis was promoted to wing commander operations of No 124 Wing. He had by this time completed almost 100 operational sorties on Typhoons – a total that would normally signal the imminent end of a frontline tour of duty – although North-Lewis would remain on operations for a further eight months. By 24 March 1945 (the day of the Rhine crossings), he had completed some 175 operational sorties, but early on that day his luck ran out when he was leading seven No 137 Sqn Typhoons on an attack on a strongpoint at Krudenberg. With his aircraft having been hit by flak, North-Lewis recalled;

'I immediately set off for the Rhine to try and make the British lines. Unfortunately, when I was over Wesel my engine stopped and I had to crash land in the first open space I could see. I made an almost perfect crash-landing and came to rest on Gravel Isle, just to the northwest of Wesel. Climbing out of my aircraft, I found I had landed within a few hundred yards of a German Parachute Regiment manning trenches on the banks of the Rhine. A German paratrooper shouted something at me, and without more ado I put my hands up.'

After an uncomfortable night, during which the Germans debated on their future actions (and their prisoner's fate!), 120 paratroopers surrendered and North-Lewis was able cross the Rhine the next morning to seek more immediate help. Returning to Helmond, he was greeted by Air Vice Marshal Harry Broadhurst, who promptly informed him that he would not be flying on operations again for some time, and that he had been awarded the DSO.

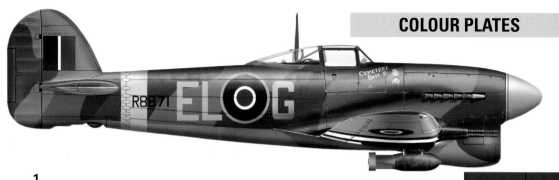

1
Typhoon IB R8871/EL-G of No 181 Sqn, No 124 Airfield, Merston, June 1943

2
Typhoon IB JP496/RD of No 121 Airfield, Westhampnett, October 1943

3
Typhoon IB JP649/ZY-Z of No 247 Sqn, No 124 Airfield, Merston, November 1943

4
36   Typhoon IB JP648/JE-D of No 195 Sqn, No 136 Wing, Fairlop, December 1943

5
Typhoon IB JP510/FM-Y of No 257 Sqn, No 146 Wing, Tangmere, March 1944

6
Typhoon IB JP535/XP-A of No 174 Sqn, No 121 Wing, Holmsley South, April 1944

7
Typhoon IB JR132/F3-F of No 438 Sqn RCAF, No 143 Wing
RCAF, Hurn, April 1944

8
Typhoon IB MN463/OV of No 197 Sqn, No 146 Wing, Needs Oar Point, May 1944

9
Typhoon IB MN454/HF-S of No 183 Sqn, No 136 Wing, Thorney Island, May 1944

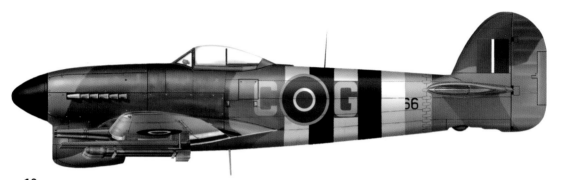

10
Typhoon IB MN666/CG of No 121 Wing, Holmsley South, June 1944

11
Typhoon IB MN353/HH-J of No 175 Sqn, No 121 Wing, Holmsley South, June 1944

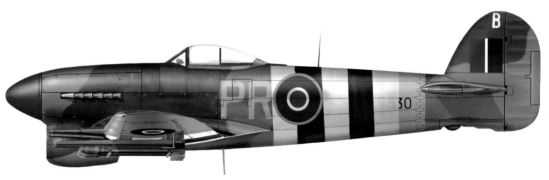

12

Typhoon IB MN630/PR-B of No 609 Sqn, No 123 Wing, Thorney Island, June 1944

13
Typhoon IB MN601/MR-K of No 245 Sqn, No 121 Wing, Holmsley South, June 1944

14
Typhoon IB MN529/BR-N of No 184 Sqn, No 129 Wing , Westhampnett and B2 Bazenville, June 1944

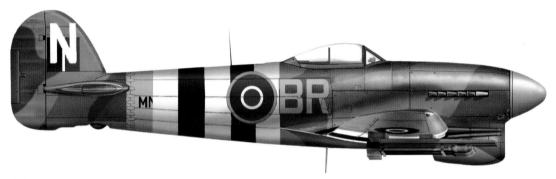

15
Typhoon IB MN413/I8-T of No 440 Sqn RCAF, No 143 Wing RCAF, B9 Lantheuil, July 1944

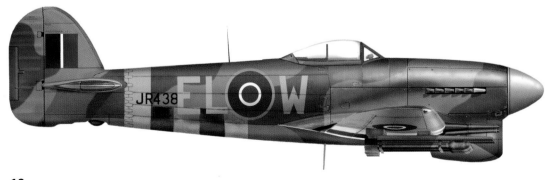

16
Typhoon IB JR438/EL-W of No 181 Sqn, No 124 Wing, B6 Coulombs, July 1944

17
Typhoon IB MN798/XM-Y of No 182 Sqn, No 124 Wing, B6 Coulombs, July 1944

18
Typhoon IB MN600/ZH-A of No 266 Sqn, No 146 Wing, B3 St Croix, August 1944

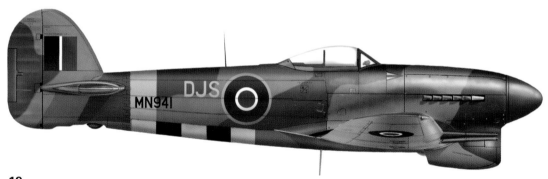

19
Typhoon IB MN941/DJS of No 123 Wing, B53 Merville, September 1944

20
Typhoon IB MN925/OV-Z of No 197 Sqn, No 146 Wing, B51 Lille-Vendeville, September 1944

21
Typhoon IB MN951/TP-A of No 198 Sqn, No 123 Wing, B53 Merville, September 1944

22
Typhoon IB MP189/KN-L of No 124 Wing, B78 Eindhoven, September 1944

23
Typhoon IB JP504/SF-R of No 137 Sqn, No 124 Wing, B78 Eindhoven, October 1944

24
Typhoon IB MN716/F3-A of No 438 Sqn RCAF, No 143 Wing RCAF, B78 Eindhoven, October 1944

25
Typhoon IB PD600/DP-C of No 193 Sqn, No 146 Wing, B70 Deurne, November 1944

26
Typhoon IB EK140/QC-K of No 168 Sqn, No 143 Wing RCAF, B78 Eindhoven, December 1944

27
Typhoon IB RB205/FGG of No 143 Wing RCAF, B78 Eindhoven, December 1944

28
Typhoon IB MN345/5V-G of No 439 Sqn RCAF, No 143 Wing RCAF, B78 Eindhoven, December 1944

29
Typhoon IB MP126/ZY-Y of No 247 Sqn, No 124 Wing, B78 Eindhoven, December 1944

30
Typhoon IB MN987/DP-T of No 193 Sqn, No 146 Wing, B70 Deurne, December 1944

31
Typhoon IB R7620/XP-P of No 174 Sqn, No 121 Wing, B80 Volkel, February 1945

32
Typhoon IB MN978/FJ-Z of No 164 Sqn, No 123 Wing, B77 Gilze-Rijen, February 1945

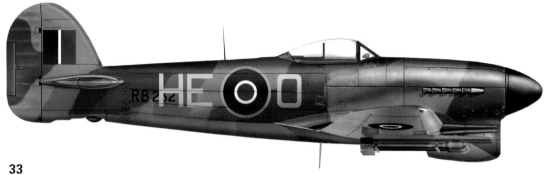

33
Typhoon IB RB232/HE-O of No 263 Sqn, No 146 Wing, B89 Mill, March 1945

34
Typhoon IB MP197/MR-U of No 245 Sqn, No 121 Wing, B80 Volkel, March 1945

35
Typhoon IB SW460/MR-Z of No 245 Sqn, No 121 Wing, B150 Hustedt, April 1945

36

Typhoon IB RB326/5V-V of No 439 Sqn RCAF, No 143 Wing RCAF, B150 Hustedt, April 1945

37
Typhoon IB RB273/DP-E of No 193 Sqn, No 146 Wing, B105 Drope, April 1945

38
Typhoon IB SW493/DP-S of No 193 Sqn, No 146 Wing, B89 Mill, April 1945

39
Typhoon IB RB431/JCB of No 123 Wing, B103 Plantlunne, April 1945

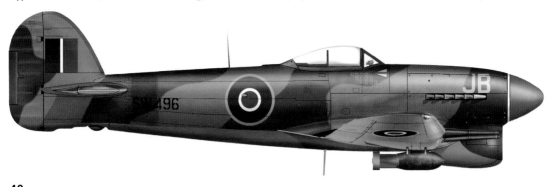

40
Typhoon IB SW496/JB of No 123 Wing, B103 Plantlunne, April 1945

BUILD-UP TO D-DAY

In the first month of its existence the new TAF had just four Typhoon squadrons – three at No 124 Airfield and one sharing No 121 Airfield accommodation with Spitfires. Few operations were flown, with units spending much of their time either organising their new tented lifestyle or participating in combined exercises with the Army. In July, however, more squadrons arrived under TAF control. Nos 174, 175 and 245 Sqns were allocated to No 121 Airfield at Lydd, while Nos 181, 182 and 247 Sqns joined No 124 Airfield at New Romney. It was the start of associations that would last for the duration of the war. Both Airfields came under the command of Grp Capt 'Paddy' Woodhouse as No 16 Wing, with Wg Cdrs Crowley-Milling and Ingle as 'Wing Leaders' of Nos 121 and 124 Airfields, respectively.

While small-scale operations such as 'Rhubarbs' (small attacks by fighters with the object of destroying enemy aircraft in the air or on the ground, or striking at ground targets) continued, more ambitious wing formations were now employed – not always with great success. One squadron at each airfield retained a 'fighter role' (Nos 245 and 247 Sqns), while the remainder carried out the bombing, frequently of enemy airfields such as Poix, Triqueville, Merville and Amiens. The Luftwaffe did not often intervene, but when it did, by virtue of height, surprise and

The first two Typhoon fighter-bomber units – Nos 181 and 182 Sqns – were both officially formed on 25 August 1942. However, they did not receive aircraft until the following month, and even then they were outdated 'second-hand' Typhoons. New-build 'bombers' were eventually received in mid-October, including R7877 for No 181 Sqn. It became EL-X, the CO's aircraft. These pilots are, from left to right, Sgts 'Vin' Vincent (later to command the squadron), 'Jimmy' Bryant (who would command No 247 Sqn), Hugh Collins and 'Billy' Grey, Flg Off 'Paddy' King, Sqn Ldr Denis Crowley-Milling and Flt Lt Tony Zweigbergk (later to command Nos 1 and 245 Sqns). Collins and King would both be shot down during the first Typhoon rocket attack on 24 October 1943. The former survived as a PoW but the latter was killed (*W Grey*)

Sqn Ldr Tom Pugh of No 182 Sqn is flanked by his two flight commanders, namely Flt Lt Jiri Manak (who would later become the only Czech to command a Typhoon squadron, No 198) and Flt Lt Bill Ireson (who would later command a Spitfire squadron, No 130). Pugh, who had earlier led a Whirlwind squadron, was killed attacking a destroyer in heavily defended Dunkirk harbour on 2 August 1943 (*No 182 Sqn records*)

Brought down by flak returning from escorting Bostons to Albert on 16 August 1943, JP577/HH-T of No 175 Sqn is seen in German hands, but its pilot was on the run. Sgt H E R Merlin certainly lived up to his name, evading the Germans, joining the Resistance, becoming a driver for the French engineer in charge of *Noball* site construction and smuggling plans of these back to the UK! When life became a bit too hot he fled to Switzerland, but bored with internment he escaped back into France and joined the Maquis. Merlin eventually rejoined his squadron at B50 Vitry-en-Artois, arriving in a captured Kubelwagen some 14 months after he was posted 'missing'! JP577 was displayed in the Luftwaffe's Sample Collection, Beutepark 5 at Paris-Nanterre (*via A S Thomas*)

perhaps experience, it usually had the upper hand. Flak and technical failure also took their toll.

Escorts to bomber operations, codenamed 'Ramrods', for No 2 Group or Ninth Air Force medium bombers were sometimes provided, and during one such mission on 19 August to Amiens No 182 Sqn lost three out of six aircraft following an encounter with fighters of II./JG 26. One of those to be shot down was Flt Lt Geoff Ball, who recalled latching onto an enemy fighter prior to his own demise;

'He rolled onto his back and tried to escape by diving, but I followed him and shot him down. God knows what speed we got up to – the ASI was "off the clock" (i.e. more than 550 mph!). The cockpit hood burst open and the propeller overspeed threw oil back all over the windscreen. I took some cine shots of "my" '109 and then started to hedgehop my way home, but I flew directly over the top of a flak post and got a belly-full. As well as the engine, I lost the rudder and had to fly straight ahead into an orchard. The aircraft hit the trees, turned over and exploded – if I had stayed the right way up I would have frizzled but, upside down, the fire was above me.'

Despite burns to his face and hands, Ball managed to struggle clear, only to be caught, along with four other evaders, within sight of the Pyrenees. He spent a harrowing six months as a 'guest' of the Gestapo.

Flg Off M I Fraleigh was shot down by the German fighters and killed, but the other No 182 Sqn loss during this combat, Flt Sgt Ron Dench, was more fortunate, bailing out and evading successfully. Returning to England in November, he subsequently resumed operational flying with No 182 Sqn. Another No 16 Wing operation that resulted in losses took place on 11 September when Grp Capt Woodhouse and Wg Cdr Alec Ingle led Nos 175, 182 and 245 Sqns on a 'Ramrod' to the Poix area.

Again, II./JG 26 Fw 190s attacked, Ingle and one of the No 175 Sqn pilots being shot down – only three claims for damage to the German aircraft were submitted in return.

That same month a significant development took place when, in early September, the first RP-equipped Typhoons were received by No 181 Sqn at New Romney. It would be several weeks before enough aircraft were available to give the pilots practice with the new weapon, but eventually the first operation took place, on 21 October. Sqn Ldr Frank Jensen led three of his pilots in search of shipping around the Channel Islands, although none was found.

Four days later, a sophisticated operation involving all six squadrons of No 16 Wing was launched. Six No 181 Sqn pilots were briefed to attack Caen power station with RPs, while No 174 Sqn, escorted by No 245 Sqn, was to provide a diversion by dive-bombing nearby marshalling yards from high level while Nos 175 and 182 Sqns made 'dummy runs' over Caen to draw the flak. The rocket-carriers, having been escorted to the target area by No 247 Sqn, were to make their run in across the marshalling yards, which would hopefully have been reduced to a shambles by the bombers. In reality, the plans went awry when cloud cover prevented the bombing. The flak, possibly alerted by signalmen as No 181 Sqn's route to Caen had been at low-level along a railway line, refused to be decoyed by the higher squadrons' antics. Sqn Ldr Frank Jensen, who was leading No 181 Sqn in two 'vics' of three, recalled;

'Just before the target was a line of poplars which marked the point where it was necessary to pull up into the rocket launching position. At that moment all Hell let loose as the flak batteries opened up. Flg Off Hugh Collins and myself were hit immediately, and Flg Off 'Paddy' King a few seconds later. I prepared for a forced landing, jettisoning my rockets and cockpit side panels. With all forward vision obscured by oil on the windscreen, I had to stick my head out the side of the cockpit, but fortunately I spotted a ploughed field on which to put the Typhoon down. I remember trying to keep the "Tiffie" straight with the rudder, as normal, and the rudder bar nearly broke my ankles.'

In the late summer of 1943 both of TAF's Typhoon Airfields operated two squadrons of fighter-bombers and a third with 'fighters'. At No 124 Airfield, it was No 247 Sqn that fulfilled this latter role. EK224/ZY-B was one of their 'fighter' Typhoons, photographed at Bradwell Bay, where No 247 Sqn spent a short period away from the TAF on anti-'Rhubarb' patrols (*C E Brayshaw*)

Repaired after this argument with a drainage ditch at the end of New Romney's runway, JP513/EL-F was flown by Sqn Ldr Frank Jensen on 'Black Monday' (25 October 1943) during the Typhoon RP attack. Hit by flak, Jensen was forced to land before reaching the target – a Caen power station (*D J Coxhead*)

Jensen and Collins were captured but King was killed. The second formation, despite Jensen's warning, carried out their attack and registered hits with all three salvoes of rockets.

EXPANSION AND *NOBALLS*

The beginning of November 1943 found RAF Fighter Command with 18 operational Typhoon squadrons on strength, but still with only six of them as yet allocated to the TAF. On the 15th of the month, Fighter Command was temporarily dissolved and the TAF became independent as the 2nd Tactical Air Force, although at first operations continued to be controlled by No 11 Group of ADGB (as the remnants of Fighter Command were known).

Early November had also seen a new target identified for the attention of Allied bombers. Construction works, many incorporating distinctive ski-shaped structures, were springing up in many areas of the Pas de Calais, and these were known to be launching sites for the new Fieseler Fi 103 pilotless flying bomb – later known as the V1 or 'Doodlebug'. Typhoons joined a host of Allied bombers in an all-out assault on these priority targets, which were soon code-named *Noballs*. The attacks, in the face of stiff opposition at some sites, were made throughout December and into the New Year, continuing until July 1944. Some Typhoon squadrons would make as many as three visits to the Pas de Calais in a single day.

After February, however, the Typhoon's participation was somewhat reduced because of the preparations for D-Day. In fact, by mid-February the Germans had realised that they were fighting a losing battle, and while maintaining token work on the original sites, they had concentrated their major effort on new, smaller and highly camouflaged sites. Indeed, it was these that were eventually used to launch the V1 campaign in June of that year.

The technique used when attacking the *Noball* targets is described here by WO Bob Betts of No 247 Sqn;

'We would approach the target, keeping radio silence, in squadron formation at 8000 ft. The anti-aircraft guns would keep silent, hoping that we had not seen the site. We would fly over the target and position for the best angle of attack, break radio silence, fuse the 500-lb bombs, fall into line astern and be prepared to dive within seconds. The angle of dive was 45 degrees, but this felt like 90 degrees in the cockpit. In the dive you

In the autumn of 1943 the TAF's 'fighter' Typhoons were converted to fighter-bombers, joining the other TAF Typhoons in the campaign against the *Noball* sites. Sqn Ldr Erik Haabjorn's JP649/ZY-Z, armed with two 500-lb bombs, displays the interim canopy improvements that enhanced the pilot's view by cleaning up the area behind his head armour (*E Haabjorn*)

had to watch the small hand (thousands of feet) of the altimeter, since the big hand (hundreds) was moving too fast, watch the ASI which would go above 550 mph, trim out any skid by keeping the needle and ball central, line the target up on the vertical red line on the gunsight and watch for other Typhoons, especially those underneath.

'On approaching 4000 ft you checked for skid once more, pulled gently back on the stick and watched as the target moved down the vertical red line of the gunsight. When it disappeared below the nose you counted up to five slowly, or ten fast, then pressed the bomb release button at the end of the throttle in your left hand. This form of attack proved to be an extremely accurate method, with an average error of less than 50 yards.'

ADGB Typhoon squadrons had pioneered long-range sweeps with some success, and these were echoed by Nos 121 and 124 Wings, but with more limited results. A noteworthy operation was undertaken on 18 February under the code-name *Jericho* – the now-famous low-level attack on the German prison at Amiens by Mosquito fighter-bombers of No 2 Group. The plan involved 18 Mosquitos from Nos 21, 464 and 487 Sqns attacking in three waves. Each wave was to have an escort of eight Typhoons, and the operation was timed for midday in order to catch many of the guards at lunch. The Typhoon escort was to be provided by Nos 174 and 245 Sqns at Westhampnett, with a third ADGB unit from Manston.

There seems to have been some failure in communications, as the briefing for the Westhampnett squadrons was carried out in great haste at 1055 hrs and the first Typhoons were airborne at 1110 hrs! There had been no time to fit the long-range tanks that were desirable for an operation of this duration.

At Manston, where the weather was appalling, with very low cloud and snowstorms, there was also confusion. A handful of Typhoons got airborne, and while some were forced to return, others found only the Film Production Unit (FPU) Mosquito and escorted that. Meanwhile, at Westhampnett, where the weather was slightly better, eight Typhoons of No 174 Sqn, led by Flt Lt 'Granny' Grantham, were followed into the air by eight more from No 245 Sqn, the latter machines being led by

For two months after No 195 Sqn had joined 2nd TAF, it was the only one Typhoon-equipped in No 84 Group. The squadron was disbanded as part of a reorganisation of the Typhoon force in February 1944. Accordingly, the aircraft shown here, JP648/JE-D, was transferred to No 164 Sqn, which was converting to Typhoons from Hurricane IVs. Its usual pilot, Flg Off Ken Trott, was posted to No 197 Sqn (*K A J Trott*)

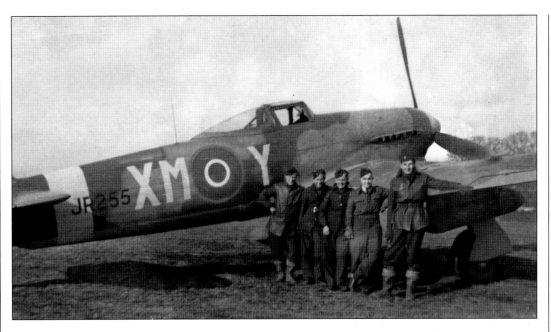

Plt Off Douglas Coxhead's No 182 Sqn groundcrew pose with his JR255/XM-Y at Merston in March 1944. Equipped with 44-gallon tanks for a long-range sortie, the aircraft is without the black and white identity stripes that had been carried by Typhoons for over a year (they would be visible on the undercarriage doors). This marking change reflected the more offensive role of the aircraft in 1944 – the stripes had been deleted from all Typhoons by 7 February 1944 to make them less visible over enemy territory (*D J Coxhead*)

Sqn Ldr J R Collins. Both these units had been briefed to rendezvous with their respective Mosquito formations over Littlehampton. The bad weather had its influence here too, but No 174 Sqn managed to meet up with four Mosquitos of the second wave (which were joined by another three in mid-Channel) and No 245 Sqn located the three Mosquitos that were all that remained of the third wave.

Flg Off H V 'Junior' Markby, an Australian flying one of the No 174 Sqn Typhoons, takes up the story;

'After crossing the French coast we descended to ground level and escorted the Mosquitos to the target, then formed a defensive circle while the bombing runs were made. There was a thin veil of cloud over the area at about 1000 ft, and this provided excellent cover for some Fw 190s that made attacks from above, breaking back into the cloud from where they could still observe our aircraft. Another pilot and myself had been delegated to stay with the FPU Mosquito, and when the other aircraft turned for home, we remained in order to prevent enemy fighters from interfering with it as its crew made several photographic runs. We were pleased to formate on him on the way home, as the weather deteriorated again and we figured he was better equipped to guide us in the IFR conditions as we were running out of fuel.'

Flg Off J E Renaud was forced to land four miles north of Amiens and was taken prisoner. At the time his loss was put down to flak, but German records reveal that his Typhoon was brought down by ace Leutnant Waldemar Radener of II./JG 26. Two Mosquitos also failed to return, including that of strike leader, Grp Capt P C Pickard DSO DFC, who was shot down by ace Leutnant Wilhelm Mayer, also of II./JG 26.

The main task, however, was still *Noballs* – and the drive to prepare for D-Day. This entailed all the squadrons taking it in turns to visit the APCs, and in the case of 11 squadrons, coming to grips with, or refining, their techniques with rockets. Many of these units received RP-equipped aircraft as late as March and April, while others would not be fully equipped

The German radar 'chimney' at De Haan, near Ostende, was selected as a trial target for rocket-Typhoons on 16 March 1944 in order to validate an attack plan for the radars in the Normandy invasion area. Seen here before (top) and during (above) the RP attack by No 198 Sqn, led by Sqn Ldr 'Johnny' Baldwin, the installation was badly damaged and had to be dismantled for repair. It was out of action for three months (*J R Baldwin*)

until May. Time was spent practising landings on small strips in preparation for those expected to be available in France. Many pilots, once they reached a reasonable level of experience, were temporarily posted out to non-operational roles, allowing newly trained pilots to replace them and acquire operational experience. Heavy casualties were expected in the battle for France.

With the attendance of so many squadrons at APCs during April, operational activity was reduced, but there was an unexpected encounter for No 266 Sqn. Returning from an early morning exercise on 18 April, four pilots were greeted by a rare sight at this stage of the war – a German bomber over the South coast in daylight! Passing over their new base (Needs Oar Point) in line astern prior to landing, the leader's attention was drawn by a series of flak bursts about a mile ahead. Their target was quickly identified as a Ju 188. Closing rapidly, the leader, Flt Lt A V Sanders, and Flt Sgt D H Dodd each made a single pass, firing 100 rounds apiece. The bomber went down immediately, and when the wreckage was investigated it was found to have seven crew (more than usual) on board. Over the years there were many 'conspiracy' theories to explain this odd event, but the cold truth is that the German crew had made a fatal navigational error in bad weather when moving up to a forward base in preparation for night operations. The extra passengers were groundcrew.

The all-Canadian No 143 Airfield became fully operational during April, Wg Cdr R T P Davidson having moved across from No 121 Airfield to lead his compatriots in the air. On 24 April one of Davidson's units, No 438 Sqn, dropped pairs of 1000-lb bombs on a bridge at St Saveur – the first time that such weapons had been released operationally by Typhoons – although due to a shortage of suitable aircraft within its wing, the unit had to use No 439 Sqn Typhoons to do it! Bombs of this size were particularly useful against bridges, and the Canadians made many such attacks in coming weeks as part of the campaign to disrupt communications in northern France.

May saw a great resurgence of activity amongst the Typhoon units directed against a variety of priority targets, including more *Noball* sites and the railway system of northwest France, but from 10 May the coastal radar network from the Pas de Calais to Brittany became the prime target. These sites were particularly difficult objectives to hit accurately and effectively. The aerials in most cases were relatively small, dispersed, protected by blast walls and very heavily defended by flak batteries of all calibres. The nature of the targets, whose destruction or severe reduction would be vital to the success of D-Day, meant that the task fell largely to the Typhoon squadrons.

Back on 16 March No 198 Sqn had established the validity of using rockets against radar sites with two attacks on the De Haan 'radar chimney', which was so badly damaged that it had to be totally dismantled for repair. Some sites, however, had to be attacked several times, with defences therefore fully alerted. The number of losses suffered by Typhoon units rose alarmingly, with a high proportion of formation leaders being shot down.

In an effort to conceal the identity of the intended invasion beaches, it was necessary to attack two sites outside that area for every one within it. During the last week before D-Day an intensive series of attacks was made on 42 sites, and finally on the last three days 12 sites selected as especially worthy of attention received last visits. Rocket Typhoons made 694 sorties, firing 4517 RPs, and a further 759 sorties were shared between bomb-equipped Typhoons and Spitfires, who dropped 1258 500 'pounders' between them.

Just before the anti-radar campaign began, on 8 May the Canadian wing lost its leader when Wg Cdr Davidson suffered an engine failure while leading an attack on Douai marshalling yards. He was forced to land in France, joining the growing list of evaders, but instead of passing along one of the escape routes, he stayed and fought with the Maquis, eventually linking up with Allied forces after the invasion. The very next day No 124 Airfield's popular Norwegian leader Erik Haabjorn had the first of two narrow escapes during May (see Chapter 3).

Meanwhile, the campaign against communications continued. Bridges of all descriptions, river and rail traffic, junctions and marshalling yards were the most common targets, but anything of military value was fair game. On 23 May Nos 193 and 257 Sqns jointly attacked a rail tunnel into which a train had just disappeared, bombing each end simultaneously and blocking them, thus sealing in their intended target. On this particular day No 257 Sqn noted a record delivery of ordnance,

Covered by straw to help conceal it from Allied fighters, JP510/FM-Y of No 257 Sqn had been forced down following engine failure while engaged in an 'offensive weather reconnaissance' on 16 March 1944. After initially evading capture Plt Off J B Wood was betrayed to the German forces. This aircraft had been Sqn Ldr 'Ronnie' Fokes' FM-A (see *Osprey Aircraft of the Aces 27 – Typhoon and Tempest Aces of World War 2*) and, unusually, had been returned to the same unit after canopy modifications. Re-coded FM-Y, it still retained Fokes' personal marking and rank pennant on the nose (*via G Rayner*)

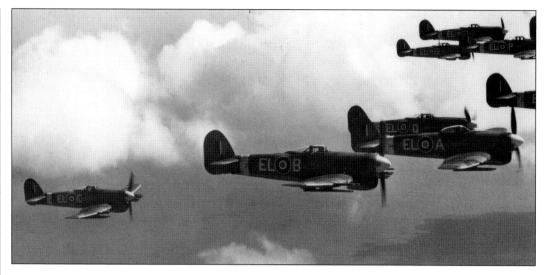

firing 9615 20 mm shells and dropping 62 500-lb bombs. No 184 Sqn paid several visits to the marshalling yards at Gamaches, which was also attacked by No 245 Sqn on 28 May. Aircraft from the former unit came up against a new hazard on this occasion – rocket-launched cables which then descended slowly by parachute. Flt Sgt D J Lush brought back 15 yards of cable trailing from his wing after it had cut 18 inches into the leading edge. No 184 Sqn had joined No 121 Airfield at Holmsley South for a week commencing 13 May, and after the invasion the unit would become a permanent member of that wing.

The radar war continued to exact its toll too, particularly among the squadron commanders. On 23 May Sqn Ldr Jimmy Keep was hit while leading No 181 Sqn in the anti-flak role over Cherbourg (see Chapter 3). No 164 Sqn's Sqn Ldr H A B Russell was forced to bail out attacking a 'Freya' site at Fruges five days later and he was posted missing. Sqn Ldr D G Ross of No 193 Sqn was also missing after bailing out nearer to home – just 15 miles off the Isle of Wight – on the eve of D-Day.

On 2 June No 198 Sqn had lost its commander, Sqn Ldr J Niblett, during a joint attack with No 609 Sqn on the nightfighter and coastal battery control radars at Caude Cote, just west of Dieppe. While four No 198 Sqn aircraft led by Niblett ran in from the sea, 12 others from both squadrons dived out of the sun. Flt Lt Denis Sweeting was Niblett's number two;

'I was looking to "Nibby's" aircraft for the lead in when it seemed to flash. It looked as if he had fired his rockets, which I thought was too early, as we had decided before take-off to fire as we crossed the cliff-top. Then, petrified with horror, I realised that his aircraft had been hit and had burst into flames. In a second all that became visible of the Typhoon was its wingtips sticking out of a ball of fire. The tips turned slowly over and the aircraft must have been on its back when it hit the base of the cliff and exploded.'

This attack was not successful, and it had to be repeated the following day. No 198 Sqn had also suffered losses during the previous month when, on 24 May, Sqn Ldr Niblett had led four Typhoons against the Jobourge site on the northwest tip of the Cherbourg peninsula.

Photographed by a No 430 Sqn RCAF Mustang I while returning from an RP strike in April 1944, this No 181 Sqn formation is comprised of an unusually varied collection of Typhoons. Only MN208/EL-A has RP and a bubble-canopy, while JR297/B, JR294/C and JR244/Q all have the interim improved canopies and RPs and JP551/S has the old canopy with an aerial mast and bomb carriers (it had probably been employed as 'fighter escort'). This situation had come about because No 181 Sqn was the first RP unit, and it had received RP-equipped aircraft over a period of several months, whereas most squadrons received new-build or modified Typhoons that had both RP and canopy modifications incorporated in a short period of re-equipment (*W Grey*)

A German PoW later described the attack as he had witnessed it from the ground;

'Three (four actually attacked) Typhoons came in from the valley, flying very low in line astern. The second aircraft got a direct hit from 37 mm flak, which practically shot off its tail. The pilot, however, managed to keep some sort of control and continued straight at the target. He dived below the level of the rim of the "Mammut's" aerial, released his rockets into the structure and then tried to climb at the last moment to clear it. The third aircraft, in trying to avoid the damaged Typhoon, touched the latter's fuselage with a wing tip. Both aircraft locked together and crashed some 100 yards beyond the target. The "Mammut" was never serviceable again.'

The Typhoons that collided had been flown by Flg Off H Freeman and Flt Sgt L Vallerly, and it is thought that the aircraft which almost hit the 'Mammut' was Freeman's. It was impossible to establish whether or not the Typhoon had been flown at the aerial deliberately, as some thought, including German witnesses. These doubts stifled discussion of the possible award of a Victoria Cross to Freeman.

One of the radar sites that was attacked during this period had the unique distinction of being on UK territory! This was the complex at Fort St George on Guernsey, and it proved a tough nut to crack. An attack by Nos 181 and 182 Sqns on 27 May was followed by a visit from all three squadrons from their wing on 2 June. Some equipment remained serviceable, so the next day No 439 Sqn plastered the site with bombs – still one stubborn 'Freya' appeared to be functioning, however. The installation received its 'coup de grace' on the eve of D-Day when No 439 Sqn paid another visit, but it cost this unit its first casualty to enemy action. The formation leader, Flt Lt J W Saville, had led eight Typhoons in a dive from 12,000 ft down to 4000 ft before releasing their bombs. Apparently Saville had been hit in the dive for he was unable to pull out.

His Majesty King George VI inspected some of 2nd TAF's latest types at Northolt on 3 May 1944. Representing rocket-Typhoons was MN454/HF-S of No 183 Sqn, wearing Sqn Ldr The Honourable Felix Scarlett's pennant. This Typhoon was one of around 200 that were built with the large 'Tempest' tailplane (note that the tailplane leading edge overlaps the pre-painted rear fuselage band), but fitted with three-bladed propellers due to a shortage of effective oil seals for the 'four-bladers' that were designed to go with the larger tailplane. Eight days after this photograph was taken, Scarlett had a near escape when MN454 was hit by flak while attacking the radar station at Cap d'Antifer. The nose fuel tank caught fire but the flames went out as Scarlett prepared to abandon the aircraft, and he was able to bring the badly damaged Typhoon back to base (*via A J Cranston*)

Few German aircraft were seen at this time, but during an armed reconnnaissance over the Gisern-Pontoise area on 18 May by Nos 164 and 183 Sqns, two Bf 109s were claimed shot down in a two-minute dogfight, Wg Cdr Bryan sharing one of these with a pilot from No 183 Sqn. In rather different circumstances on the 29th, Flg Off 'Neufy' Taylor and another pilot from No 183 Sqn were scrambled from Thorney Island after a pair of raiders. Taylor caught the Bf 109 fighter-bombers and rapidly despatched both with the expenditure of just 20 rounds per gun.

The three RCAF squadrons of No 143 Wing attended No 16 APC at Hutton Cranswick during mid-May for their week of instruction – they were the last to undertake such a course before the great day. By the beginning of June the Canadians were also practising the art of smoke-laying. Two other Typhoon bomber units (Nos 197 and 266 Sqns) had also undergone training in this role, but these skills were never put to the test for it was decided that the Typhoons could not be spared from their primary roles.

By the eve of D-Day the intense operations of May and early June had cost the 2nd TAF 46 Typhoons lost in action or accidents, 23 pilots killed, six captured and three still busy evading capture. Most of the losses had come in the offensive against the German radar network, which had been expensive in terms of the losses suffered by the Typhoon wings, but extremely effective in respect to the fact that it had effectively blinded the enemy in the run up to the invasion.

All six long-range aircraft reporting stations south of Boulogne had been destroyed and at least 15 other installations in the area were rendered

Photographed after the invasion, this German 'Giant Wurzburg' fighter control radar had received attention from Typhoon rockets and cannon fire (*J R Baldwin*)

unserviceable. Large stretches of the French Channel coast were therefore without their normal radar coverage. It was calculated that on the night of the invasion there was never more than 18 percent of the radar in northwest France in operation, and at times it was as little as five percent. The Germans did not receive the early warning that the radar should have given them. This meant that no fighters interfered with the potentially vulnerable airborne operations, the coastal batteries were impotent, the enemy was totally confused about just how large the invasion force was and vital decisions were delayed when it came to mobilising reinforcements to defend the Normandy beaches. Thousands of Allied lives were saved as a result.

On 3 June orders were received to paint the famous 'Invasion stripes' on the Typhoons (and on all Allied aircraft operating in the area for that matter). This was accomplished by the next day. All was now ready, bar the weather, and on 5 June 1944 the RAF's Typhoon units were disposed as follows;

2nd TAF

No 83 Group

No 121 Wing
Holmsley South
Nos 174, 175 and 245 Sqns

No 124 Wing
Hurn
Nos 181, 182 and 247 Sqns

No 129 Wing
Westhampnett
No 184 Sqn

No 143 Wing
Hurn
Nos 438, 439 and 440 Sqns

No 84 Group

No 123 Wing
Thorney Island
Nos 198 and 609 Sqns

No 136 Wing
Thorney Island
Nos 164 and 183 Sqns

No 146 Wing
Needs Oar Point
Nos 193, 197, 257 and 266 Sqns

NORMANDY

When the long-awaited day dawned – D-Day, 6 June 1944 – 18 Typhoon squadrons were available to the 2nd TAF, with nine allotted to the 'Air Alert role'. Employed three at a time, one squadron was allocated to each of the three British and Canadian Assault Forces.

The honour of being first in over the invasion beaches fell to the three Canadian squadrons of No 143 Wing, their arrival being timed to coincide with the approach of the first landing craft at H-hour – 0725 hrs. The pilots were briefed to call the HQ ships on arrival in case the Assault Force commanders required them to take on more urgent targets, but in the absence of new instructions, they dive-bombed the pre-arranged targets, which were strong points at Le Hamel and La Riviere (Gold beach), Courseulles-sur-Mer (Juno beach) and Hermanville (Sword beach). Flg Off James H Beatty was flying with No 440 Sqn;

'Twelve aircraft were used and the pilots were briefed the night before – everyone was confined to the airfield. I believe that we were the only aircraft, during the initial assault, allowed below the cloud base. Indeed, the only others we saw at our elevation were two Focke-Wulf fighters, and they climbed into the clouds. At the briefing we had been given our targets, and we were told that if we were hit we had to bail out over the Channel and the odds were that we would land on a ship. The briefing officers also suggested that we land on an empty one headed for England!

'We went into the initial target in line astern and bombed at low-level with delayed-action bombs. We then went behind the beaches after the gun positions. The visibility was very poor due to weather, smoke and dust, so it was difficult to assess results.'

The remaining nine Typhoon units not on Air Alert also had pre-arranged targets to attack, and these included four more gun sites and two Wehrmacht HQs – Chateau Le Parc, southeast of Bayeux, and Chateau La Meauffe near St Lô. Personal attention from the Typhoon wings to German HQs would be a feature of the campaign.

During the day, calls for assistance resulted in attacks on a radar station near Le Havre, which had been directing coastal guns, and strong points met by the advancing Allies. By late morning it was apparent that there were not enough targets in the assault area to keep the Typhoon force fully occupied, so some squadrons were redirected onto 'armed recces' of the area south of Bayeux, Caen and Lisieux, with their purpose being to disrupt the

Climbing away from Thorney Island, Flg Off R F Royston takes MN630/PR-B of No 609 Sqn on its second sortie on D-Day – hunting 'MET' (mechanised enemy transport) in the Lisieux area. It had earlier been flown by Flt Lt E R A Roberts in a strike against a radar station at Le Havre (*No 609 Sqn records*)

movement of reinforcements. While No 183 Sqn was thus engaged its pilots, absorbed with positioning for an attack on a tank column, failed to see the 'bounce' by a reported 12 Bf 109s (probably Fw 190s from JG 2) and three Typhoons went down with the loss of all three pilots.

Throughout the afternoon the Typhoons continued with the 'armed recces', scarcely hindered by the Luftwaffe, although No 183 Sqn's sister unit in No 136 Wing, No 164 Sqn, was also surprised by Fw 190s as they reformed after attacking vehicles. Sqn Ldr Percy Beake was leading the unit, and he later reported;

'Breaking hard, I saw one of these aircraft firing at a member of my section and, continuing to turn hard right, I was able to give the enemy fighter a short burst from his starboard quarter. The Hun immediately broke off his attack and commenced a diving turn, emitting smoke from the engine.'

Lining up for a second attack, Beake was dismayed to find that he had expended all his ammunition. However, one of his pilots saw the Fw 190 dive into the ground and explode in flames. One Typhoon failed to return, but this aircraft had been hit by flak shortly before the combat and the ultimate cause of its loss was not known.

By dusk on 6 June the Typhoon wings had flown 400 sorties for the cost of eight aircraft and pilots (although one of the latter successfully evaded). Four had gone down to enemy fighters and four to ground fire or debris damage. Resistance had been much lighter than expected, but the next day would be a rather different story.

Dawn on the 7th revealed a solid cloud base between 1500 ft and 3000 ft, but the Typhoons were airborne at first light nevertheless. No 83 Group squadrons were assigned to the area Caen-Mezidon-Falaise to a point south of Villers-Bocage, while No 84 Group patrolled the area east of this as far as Evreux. To allow sufficient time on patrol, the rocket squadrons carried long-range tanks and a reduced load of four RPs, while the bomber units had a tank under one wing and a bomb under the other. Much execution was done, particularly on unarmoured vehicles, but this work was hampered by the low cloud that forced the Typhoons to fly within easy range of light flak – this was reflected in the losses suffered. Out of a total of 493 sorties flown during the day, some of which were diverted to give direct support, 15 Typhoons were lost.

Hardest hit were Nos 184 and 245 Sqns, both of which had three aircraft destroyed. All the Typhoons lost by the former unit were shot down in one action. Flt Lt 'Dutch' Holland, who was leading a formation of eight aircraft, was one of those forced to abandon his fighter;

'We flew over Mezidon marshalling yard at approximately 1000 ft and attacked on a reciprocal course. The marshalling yard was full of tanks, anti-aircraft guns, military vehicles and troops. Everything in the world seemed to open up at us, and I was hit before we started the attack. I led the squadron down to 300 ft, at which point I was close enough to see the eyes of the gunners, and fired my rockets into the vehicles. With the satisfaction of seeing the rockets explode among them, I pulled up – my altimeter showed 200 ft – and waited for things to happen.

'As my aircraft began to falter I gave instructions for the squadron to carry on as I was bailing out. I pulled up to 1200 ft, at which point I could see fire coming from the starboard side of the fuselage. Things were getting very hot. I got my feet on the dashboard and undercarriage lever and pushed at the hood with all the force I knew. The next thing I knew I had hit the tail with my parachute and done a somersault – I remember seeing my aeroplane hit the ground before the 'chute opened.'

After 70 days on the run, 'Dutch' Holland reached Allied lines, but two of his pilots who were also hit in the attack were less fortunate, one dying when his aircraft crashed and the other bailing out into captivity.

With the beachhead established, Typhoon operations continued in the pattern set on the 7th. On that date work had commenced on the construction of the first landing grounds in France. Runways were bulldozed from the Normandy farmland and ditches and hedges levelled and surfaced with 'SMT' – steel mesh tracking. The first off these, given B (British) identification numbers, were ready for use on 10 June.

Three operations were laid on that day against two German Army HQs in an attempt to thwart counter-attacks which were about to be launched. Two of the attacks against what was thought to be the HQ of the 1st SS Panzer Corps were without success. However, during the evening 42 Typhoons from the three units of No 124 Wing at Hurn, plus No 245 Sqn from nearby Holmsley South, rocketed the Panzer *Gruppe* West's HQ at Chateau La Caine, 12 miles southwest of Caen. They were followed by 71 Mitchells bombing from 12,000 ft.

The Chateau itself was not badly damaged but the orchard sheltering the HQ's vehicles was saturated with direct hits. The Chief of Staff, General Von Dawans, and several of his officers died, and the HQ was out of action until 28 June. Perhaps more importantly, the plans for the imminent armoured counter-attack, that could have been fatal to the Allied beachhead, were literally in ashes. Later in the month, on 27 June, No 146 Wing joined the Mitchells for a similar attack on the HQ of Leutnant General Dohlman's infantry division in the St Lô area. Once again the target was destroyed and Dohlman was killed. No general was safe in his HQ in this campaign.

SHELLS AND DUST

Only seven days after D-Day the Typhoons of Nos 121, 124 and 129 Wings began using the new strips in Normandy (B2 and B3) to refuel and rearm during the day, returning to their South Coast airfields at night. This was an important development, as previously the Typhoons had had limited time over the battle area, or a little longer at the expense of a reduced bomb or RP load. It also meant that pilots of damaged aircraft were no longer faced with a lengthy Channel crossing of around 100 miles. Since the beginning of the 'radar war', 14 Typhoon pilots had bailed out or ditched in the Channel, but only nine had been rescued.

At last, on 17 June, the Normandy strips were ready to accept more permanent visitors. Dakotas delivered the ground echelon of No 121 Wing's No 174 Sqn to B5, which was scheduled as that wing's new base. However, heavy shelling forced a temporary move to B2. Three days later No 175 Sqn moved into B3, while the whole of No 124 Wing, plus No 245 Sqn, settled in on B6. On the latter strip there were now 65 Typhoons little more than three miles from the frontline.

During the evening of 21 June a Bf 109 flew over B6 at just 50 ft, obviously on a 'recce ' run. No 245 Sqn's diarist remarked 'we shall be

On the morning of 10 June 1944, MN601/MR-K became the first aircraft to make a wheels-down landing at the first strip to become operational in France, B3 Ste Croix-sur-Mer. It was flown in by Flg Off W Smith (right) of No 245 Sqn after being hit by flak, which caused the engine to vibrate badly. When MR-K came to a halt on B3, Smith was met by a swarm of photographers and 'brass', who were expecting to greet Air Vice Marshal Harry Broadhurst in his Spitfire! Ten days later, Smith, who went on to command No 184 Sqn, had to make a forced landing in MN625/MR-B (above) due to engine failure – possibly a result of Normandy dust problems (*Canadian Forces/N Wilson*)

shelled or bombed soon, and this will be expensive with no blast shelters for the aircraft'. He was right. Salvoes started arriving on the morning of the 22nd, and by 1030 hrs the Typhoons had been ordered back across the Channel! By then all the squadrons had suffered severely, No 247 Sqn, for example, flying back 14 aircraft of which only four were unscathed, and leaving four unflyables at B6 – these were all eventually repaired, however, and only No 181 Sqn suffered a single write-off.

This return to UK bases was a blessing in disguise for it enabled frantic engineering activity to be carried out at Hurn and Holmsley South as Sabre engines damaged by the scouring Calvados dust were hastily replaced and all aircraft fitted with air filters (see Chapter 1). Ready to tackle the dusty conditions of Normandy, and with the shelling much reduced, the Typhoons returned to France to rejoin the groundcrews that had, in the meantime, had to sit it out. By the end of June all the No 83 Group wings were in Normandy, No 121 Wing being established at B5,

No 124 Wing at B6 and No 143 Wing at B9 – the latter wing, arriving on the 27th, was the first equipped with Typhoon bombers to be based in France. They were joined on the last day of the month by the first of the No 84 Group wings, No 123, which arrived at B10.

Since 6 June the 2nd TAF had lost nearly 70 Typhoons in action, with well over half of them falling to ground fire of one sort or another. Little more than half-a-dozen had fallen victim to German fighters, however, while claims by Typhoon pilots against the latter totalled nine.

Of these, no less than five were claimed in one engagement that took place on 29 June. Wg Cdr Baldwin of No 146 Wing was leading ten aircraft of No 193 Sqn that were covering RP Typhoons when several Bf 109s were sighted near Conches airfield. Giving orders to jettison long-range tanks, he led the Typhoons into the attack, but then a further formation of Bf 109s appeared through the clouds behind the Typhoons. A dogfight immediately developed in and out of cloud. After downing two himself, and damaging a third, Baldwin found there were now large numbers of enemy aircraft milling around, so he called on his pilots to make use of cloud cover and return individually. This they did successfully, although two damaged Typhoons were forced to land at A3 and B2. In addition to Baldwin's claims (which brought his confirmed total to 14.5), three more Bf 109s were claimed destroyed and three damaged.

The prolonged V1 flying bomb assault on southern England led to some diversion of effort from targets in Normandy during July, with 2nd TAF fighter-bombers frequently flying north to attack the launching sites during the month. Remaining coastal radar stations were also put back on the target list. When coupled with the primary ground support duties, as the armies in the beachhead struggled to break out with a succession of offensives around the Caen area, the month proved busy for the

By D+7 the rocket-Typhoons of Nos 121 and 124 Wings were using the ALGs in Normandy to refuel and rearm, but returning to UK bases at night. Here, armourers slide RPs onto the rails of MN317/ZY-B of No 247 Sqn at B2 Bazenville. This unit was a named squadron – 'China-British' – after donations made by the British community in China, and MN317 carries the title on its nose cowling, above the exhaust stubs (*via No 247 Sqn Association*)

Typhoons once again, although thankfully not as costly as had June – less than 60 aircraft were lost on operations during this month.

The arrival in Normandy of the first No 84 Group squadrons had been brief, for within days No 123 Wing had been forced to return to Hurn due to B10 having become waterlogged following heavy rain. The airstrip was also coming under regular shellfire. Nos 136 and 146 Wings also moved to Hurn, occupying dispersals left vacant by Nos 121 and 143 Wings and thus consolidating all the group's close support aircraft at this single airfield for a week or so. B15 was now used as a forward refuelling base until the units once again began moving over to the Normandy airfields on a more permanent basis. By mid-July both No 84 Group wings were established in Normandy, No 123 at B7 and No 146 at B3. In No 83 Group, No 129 Wing was disbanded, its lone Typhoon unit, No 184 Sqn, joining No 121 Wing.

All five remaining Typhoon wings were now operating from a very small area indeed, and the crowded strips and airspace overhead were still targeted by occasional shelling and strafing German fighters. Even without the presence of the enemy, dust made aircraft movements hazardous despite the liberal spraying of dispersal areas, taxiways and runways with old oil.

It is not surprising, therefore, that there were a number of accidents, one of the more serious occurring on 7 July at B6. Flt Lt J K Allison of No 181 Sqn had been hit by flak during a sortie but he had made it back to base. A serious leg wound left him unable to control his damaged Typhoon adequately during his landing and the aircraft ran into a group of eight fully armed aircraft of No 247 Sqn that were parked ready for the next sortie. Immediately the aircraft began to burn. While groundcrew and pilots hurriedly manoeuvred the doomed Typhoons so that their rockets pointed in relatively harmless directions and taxied others to safety, Flt Lt Harboard of Flying Control, aided by LAC Eason, braved the flames to drag clear the unfortunate Allison, who survived with burns. Harboard subsequently received the MBE for his bravery. Despite exploding rockets, cannon shells, flares and petrol, their prompt action had kept No 247 Sqn's losses down to three aircraft.

Throughout July and into August the round of 'armed recces' and pre-assigned strikes continued, targets varying from the keenly-sought tanks and transports, to troop concentrations or ammunition dumps merely identified by map references given to the pilots prior to them taking off. Sometimes the results were spectacular, as on 1 August when several formations were instructed to attack tank concentrations in the Bois du Homme. The attacking pilots could only claim three damaged, but the next day the Army found that 30 tanks had been destroyed, of which 20 were credited to the Typhoons.

While close support was the primary consideration, interdiction was also becoming increasingly importance. As Spitfires patrolled overhead to keep the Luftwaffe off

Few 2nd TAF Typhoon pilots were presented with air combat opportunities, but one who took what few chances came his way was No 193 Sqn's Flg Off Mike Bulleid. On 29 June 1944, Bulleid was credited with a Bf 109 destroyed in a dogfight over Conches. His next opportunity did not occur until Christmas Day when No 193 Sqn covered other Typhoons from No 266 Sqn on a train reconnaissance in the Duigen-Dortmund area. A large force of Bf 109s and Fw 190s attacked, Bulleid claiming one of the latter shot down in flames. The last Typhoon kill of the war, a Bv 138 flying boat on 3 May 1945, was officially credited to 12 pilots of No 193 Sqn, but it was Mike Bulleid's opening burst of fire that sealed the aircraft's fate (*Bulleid family*)

Domestic accommodation for Typhoon pilots in Normandy was a tent – these are No 174 Sqn's at B5 Le Fresne-Camilly. Most residents dug shallow trenches inside the tent that were deep enough to provide cover from enemy shelling for a camp-bed and its occupant (*E Little*)

Groundcrew of No 6181 Servicing Echelon take advantage of the good weather at B6 Coulombs in July 1944 – although on occasions storms turned the accustomed dust to mud. JR438/EL-W (top) was usually flown by Australian Flg Off Jack Rendall. A rather smarter Typhoon at B6 at about the same time was Flg Off Douglas Coxhead's MN798/XM-Y (bottom) of No 182 Sqn. Typical of the Typhoons that had been reaching the squadrons since around D-Day, it had a four-bladed propeller and 'Tempest' tailplane (*P E Tickner and D J Coxhead*)

the backs of the ground attack aircraft, and Mustang IIIs flew far into the interior to hit convoys on their way to the frontline, the Typhoons concentrated their efforts against the zone immediately behind the battle area to prevent the build-up of men and materiel and re-supply of the defenders.

A new tactic, first employed in the 2nd TAF on 17 July was destined to be widely used and made famous by Typhoons – Visual Control Post (VCP), better known as 'cab-rank'. The VCP was usually an armoured car in the frontline manned by a Forward Air Controller and an Army Liaison Officer, both of whom were in radio contact with the 'cab-rank' of patrolling fighter-bombers and local Army units, respectively. Flt Lt Tom Hall, who used this system many times during his tour with No 175 Sqn, describes how it worked;

'Direct support for the Army was controlled by a VCP with the advancing troops. In our aircraft we carried gridded maps, and an initial indication of the target's location was given by reference to these. When we arrived at the scene the Forward Air Controller would indicate where the rockets were to be placed by firing mortar shells, which gave off coloured smoke, at the target. When organising the attack, you had to take into account the position of the sun, the surface wind and the respective positions of the troops according to the "bomb-line" (i.e. the line between the two armies, which was quite theoretical at times). And you had to be wary of the Germans firing similarly coloured smoke shells on our boys as soon as our own smoke shells had indicated their target.'

The system worked well, and it allowed very close support to be given with relative safety.

July saw two sustained engagements with the Luftwaffe, both with the same German unit – I./JG 5. On 13th Wg Cdr Baldwin led a trio of No 197 Sqn aircraft on an armed reconnaissance towards the Seine, No 257 Sqn following close behind to attack rail yards at Verneuil. One of the No 197 Sqn pilots, Plt Off Ken Trott, spotted a half-track and requested permission to attack;

'I went down with Johnny Rook and we both attacked the half-track with cannon fire. I then heard Wg Cdr Baldwin call on the R/T to the effect that they were in the middle of about 30 '109s. We climbed to about 4000 ft and met the '109s as they popped in and out of cloud. I made one attack and then turned to make a head-on attack against another '109. This proved fatal as we collided and I was thrown out of my

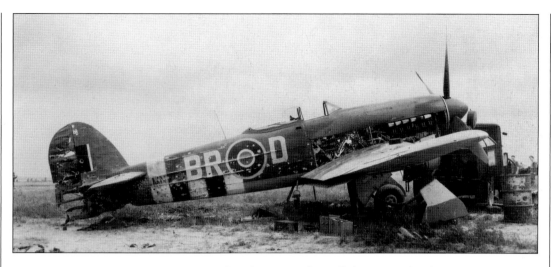

On 15 July a rocket being loaded onto a Typhoon at a B5 dispersal was inadvertently fired, passing through the cab (fortunately unoccupied) of a nearby fuel bowser (fortunately before the fuse had become live) and then being deflected by a hedge to strike the ground just short of this No 184 Sqn aircraft, MN757/BR-D. Blast and shrapnel severely damaged the rear fuselage and tail unit of the Typhoon, which was sent back to the UK for repair. It returned to service (with No 181 Sqn) some three months later (*via S Bond*)

aircraft at about 2500 ft. I pulled my ripcord and passed out. I came to hanging from a tree with several Germans standing round.'

While Ken Trott was attacking his Bf 109, Flg Off Johnny Rook had latched on to one that was glued to Trott's tail;

'As I was about to enter cloud I was hit in the rear fuselage by 20 mm ground fire. I broke away to avoid this, and not seeing any further aircraft, I decided to return to base. I came down out of cloud and was suddenly bounced by a '109. The first I knew of the attack was seeing 20 mm fire passing my cockpit and hitting the wings. I threw all the controls into one corner and opened the throttle wide with full fine pitch. The engine responded perfectly, and I screamed round after the '109 and saw him suddenly stall and spin off. By this time I was so close to the ground I am sure he went straight into the deck.'

Although outnumbered, the Typhoon pilots had fought back, Wg Cdr Baldwin and Flt Sgt A Shannon of No 257 Sqn each claiming a Bf 109 shot down, while the latter unit claimed one more probable and four damaged. No 257 Sqn also lost a Typhoon, Flt Sgt M E Marriot bailing out into captivity. He was, however, liberated when Bayeux fell to the Allies.

Six days later I./JG 5, accompanied by elements of JG 1, was out in the evening over the St Quentin-Le Havre-Bernay area when Typhoons were again seen below. This time it was another No 146 Wing unit, No 266 Sqn, out on an armed reconnaissance to the Lisieux area. The fighter-bombers were taken badly by surprise, with three Typhoons and their pilots lost, while Plt Off I H Forrester managed to claim a single victory in return.

Between these two combats, on 17 July, the German Supreme Commander in the West, General Feldmarschall Erwin Rommel, was severely injured, suffering a fractured skull when his staff car was strafed and driven off the road by British fighters. Responsibility for this attack remains disputed, with claims by No 193 Sqn, led by Wg Cdr Baldwin, widely publicised at the time. However, Spitfires from No 602 Sqn, led by the South African ace Sqn Ldr 'Chris' Le Roux, were credited post-war. It has to be said that Baldwin's claimed staff car was nowhere near the area where Rommel was injured – it was not evident that the legendary general had only been wounded at the time either. Claimants continue to surface, including Typhoons of No 266 Sqn, a Canadian Spitfire pilot and even Ninth Air Force P-47s!

'DAY OF THE TYPHOON'

Early morning mists on 7 August obscured the first movements of a full-scale German counter-attack in the countryside around Mortain.

Spearheaded by five Panzer divisions, the attack was opposed by only two US infantry divisions. By midday the mists had cleared, but the 2nd SS Panzer Division had taken Mortain, while the Wehrmacht's 2nd Panzer Division had captured three key villages, threatening to cut off Gen George Patton's US 3rd Army as it began moving into Brittany.

Forewarned of the counter-offensive by the highly secret 'Ultra' intelligence (from decoded German signals traffic), the Allied commanders were content to draw the German forces, and particularly their armour, into a trap of their own making. It was agreed, in advance, that as USAAF tactical support aircraft were mainly equipped to carry bombs, the 2nd TAF's rocket-firing Typhoons would attack the armour while the US Ninth Air Force would restrict its own fighter-bombers to enemy transport moving to and from the battle zone. 'Wingco' operations of No 121 Wing, Charles Green, was despatched by the No 83 Group HQ to pinpoint the German thrust. He later recalled;

'I was informed of a large movement of armour going towards Mortain to cut off the Americans along the coast, and decided to take a section of four up. I found low cloud over the whole area, but eventually found a small gap in the cloud. This enabled me to go down with my No 2 to investigate. My No 2 remained circling above me whilst I went down to treetop level, where I was amazed to see a whole contingent of tanks, trucks, guns and transport. This enormous line of artillery was about five miles long, nose to tail. I immediately attacked the column head-on.

'In the meantime, I had called my No 2 to come in from the rear to make his attack. After a successful hit we returned to the rest of the section, detailing them to make the attack, but to stay in the area until a further section arrived from the airfield. I then alerted group HQ and advised the whole wing to be on standby, and sections to take off at ten-minute intervals.'

No 174 Sqn was the first airborne, departing B5 at 1215 hrs, with No 181 Sqn from B6 following just ten minutes later. The pilots spotted 50 or 60 tanks and 200 vehicles lining the road from

After the battle of Normandy the countryside was littered with wreckage, among which were many Typhoons. Some of the latter were still there as late as 1947, including MN600/ZH-A of No 266 Sqn. The aircraft was hit by flak on 9 August 1944 during an 'armed-recce' of the Falaise area, and its pilot, Flt Sgt P C Green, force-landed ten miles northeast of the town. He managed to avoid capture (*via L Viton*)

Dispersed along the perimeter of B5 Le Fresne-Camilly, this No 174 Sqn Typhoon shows how the D-Day stripes were toned down when the Typhoons were based in France. This aircraft was in service with No 174 Sqn on 6 June 1944, and it would have had full stripes. These have been totally removed from the fuselage, being replaced by newly painted stripes under the fuselage – these are less than the regulation size, as each one should have been 18 inches wide – the same width as the rear fuselage band. The stripes have also been removed from the uppersurface of the wings (*E Little*)

One of the Typhoon casualties of the Mortain battle was MN459/MR-R. Five days after its loss came the news that Flt Lt Bob Lee had been found alive, albeit seriously wounded and very weak, still in the wreckage of his Typhoon. Wounded by flak, he had passed out and lost control of his Typhoon as he was attempting to force-land. The aircraft had ploughed into the ground inverted, trapping him in the cockpit. It lay in a field that was 'no-man's land', and as Lee sank in and out of consciousness, the aircraft was used for target practice by the Germans – he was hit in the leg and hand by rifle bullets. At one point a fire started, but fortunately it spluttered out. After five days a US Army battlefield clearance team found the wreck and pulled the emaciated Lee, barely alive, from the cockpit (*J-P Benamou*)

St Barthelemy to Cherence. Using classic fighter-bomber tactics, they halted the column by attacking the lead and rear vehicles, and then set about those in between. Meanwhile, another two squadrons were getting airborne, and by 1400 hrs a 'shuttle-service' had developed, with another squadron of Typhoons in the air every 20 minutes seeking their targets, making their attack and returning to refuel and rearm.

The brunt of the sorties were made by No 83 Group units, especially those of Nos 121 and 124 Wings. Although No 84 Group Typhoons made some sorties to Mortain, their main task remained attacking targets along the rest of the front. Here, aided by No 124 Wing units diverted from Mortain, they dealt with another Panzer attack at Vire.

Flak was not as bad as that frequently experienced from prepared positions, and losses in the Mortain area amounted to just five aircraft, with one pilot killed and one seriously injured. The latter had a miraculous escape. Flt Lt Bob Lee of No 245 Sqn was hit by flak and lost consciousness, and when he came round he found that his Typhoon had ploughed into the ground upside down in no-man's land. Lee managed to release his harness, but was trapped in his aircraft, where he was to spend the next five days. During that time the Germans used the wreck for target practice, unwittingly hitting him in the hand and leg, and on one occasion a fire started, but fortunately it soon went out. Just in time, Lee was found by a US unit clearing the battlefield when they pulled the Typhoon from the grave it had dug for itself, and almost for its pilot.

When darkness fell 305 Typhoon sorties had been launched during a period of some ten hours. It had been a tremendous effort by Nos 121 and 124 Wings in particular, and in addition to the endeavours of the pilots, the day-long, non-stop toil of the groundcrews, who struggled under a hot sun, assembling and loading RP and 20 mm ammunition, refuelling, servicing and sometimes patching up the Typhoons should receive due credit. At the end of the momentous day the following claims for enemy tanks had been made;

	Destroyed	Damaged
No 121 Wing	53	40
No 124 Wing	31	14
Other units	6	5

Claims for the less glamorous, but equally important, 'MET' (mechanised enemy transport) were surprisingly lower;

	Destroyed	Damaged
No 121 Wing	28	39
No 124 Wing	23	14
Other units	5	1

Shortly after this event both Army and 2nd TAF Operational Research Sections studied the battleground to assess the results actually achieved. These studies cast considerable doubt on the claims made by the pilots at the time, the investigations concluding that 17 vehicles (seven of them tanks) had clearly been destroyed by rocket strikes, 14 by cannon or machine gun fire from the air and two by bombs. Fourteen had been abandoned intact (seven tanks) and five more destroyed by their crews (four tanks). US Army fire had destroyed 38 more (including 19 tanks and a self-propelled gun), while 42 (including four tanks and two self-propelled guns) had succumbed to unidentified causes. Thus total vehicular losses that could be found and categorised amounted to 132, 43 of which were tanks, three self-propelled guns, 23 armoured troop carriers, eight armoured cars, four artillery pieces, an armoured recovery vehicle and 50 various 'soft-skinned' vehicles.

How can the pilots' claims be rationalised against these results, and why, if the Typhoons were not hitting their targets in the numbers claimed, were the attacks so obviously effective? There is no doubt the rocket projectile was an inaccurate weapon, with 'weather cocking' and 'trajectory drop' built-in problems, but the slightest 'slip', 'skid' or G at the moment of launch, not to mention the pilot's estimation of range, could cause substantial error. The results of attacks could not be supported by 'combat film' as an aircraft had usually pulled out of its dive prior to the rockets arriving at their targets. Estimates of the effectiveness of attacks had to be made by the pilot as he climbed and turned away, often under heavy fire, from a smoke and dust obscured battlefield.

In a chaotic action like Mortain, as in air combat, different aircraft could shoot at the same target and each believe the results were their own. Furthermore, in ground attack, vehicles that had already been knocked out, but not destroyed, could be attacked again. The losses inspected were, of course, also only those left on the battlefield, and did not take account of any damaged units removed by the German recovery service.

Yet the attacks had obviously been decisive. The accuracy and effectiveness of the 20 mm cannons had proved a very significant factor in destroying the 'soft-skinned' vehicles bringing forward fuel and ammunition, but perhaps the most significant factor was a phenomenon observed at Mortain and subsequently employed to advantage during the rest of the campaign in northwest Europe. Both the attacking pilots and the defending US soldiers reported being greatly impressed by the apparent impact of their attacks on the morale of the German troops, who were seen to abandon their vehicles and scramble for cover in the surrounding woods and hedgerows. Interrogation of PoWs showed them to be extremely

Opened like a sardine tin, this Panzer IV was hit in the rear decking by a rocket fired from a Typhoon (*via J-P Benamou*)

nervous of RP attack, despite the fact that the chances of them being directly hit by a rocket were relatively small.

Certainly many tanks were abandoned when under attack, despite having suffered only superficial damage. There can be little doubt that an attack by a fighter-bomber (particularly one firing RPs) appeared to the soldier on the ground to have a very personal element to it – much more so than is attributable to the more impersonal impact of artillery or mortar fire. Again and again it was the evidence provided by the Germans themselves that indicated how devastatingly effective the presence of the fighter-bomber was in paralysing their activities, regardless of the actual damage that they proved capable of inflicting. In many ways this was the Typhoon's greatest contribution to the battles in which it took part.

As far as the situation at Mortain is concerned, the Typhoons had been the weapon that halted the panzers and destroyed German hopes of a successful counter-attack. At 1940 hrs on 7 August a signal from the Chief of Staff of the 7th German Army was intercepted. The latter had been forced to admit that the attack had been at a standstill since 1300 hrs due to the 'employment of fighter-bombers by the enemy and the absence of our own air support'. The Mortain action – the 'Day of the Typhoon' – was probably the most decisive tactical air operation of the invasion, and possibly the campaign in northwest Europe, as it showed the flexibility and economy of the fighter-bomber, its ease of control and the weight of fire that it could quickly bring to bear on any threatened point.

Coupled with the long, slogging battle with which the British and Canadian armies had held the main German forces further north, the defeat at Mortain put a virtual end to the defence of Normandy. Following up General Feldmarschall Günther Von Kluge's retreating forces, the US 1st Army moved forward, making contact with the British 2nd Army on its left. There was now a strong possibility of surrounding the German 7th Army, and Field Marshal Bernard Montgomery ordered the Canadians to attack again on 14 August in an effort to meet Patton's spearheads at Argentan. 2nd TAF close support aircraft headed the Canadian attack, while Bomber Command raided Falaise, almost reducing the town to a heap of impassable rubble.

By the 18th only a small gap remained at Chambois, where the Germans fought desperately to prevent the 'pocket' being closed. Now the fighter-bombers came into their own again, and for the rest of the month the 7th Army's columns, trapped in the narrow lanes of Normandy, were repeatedly attacked and the most fearful carnage caused. The density of ground fire above the packed targets was very heavy, however, and Typhoon losses during August were to reach an all-time high for the war, with more than 90 aircraft lost on operations and many others damaged. Peak losses occurred on 18 August when 17 Typhoons failed to return and a dozen pilots were killed.

All day on the 18th the Allied fighter-bombers poured a murderous hail of bombs, rockets, cannon and machine gun fire on the German forces massed in the jaws of the gap between Trun and Chambois. By late afternoon hundreds of military vehicles of all kinds were forming huge jams outside Vimoutiers, and the No 83 Group Typhoons zeroed in on this area. Soon the roads were blocked by blazing trucks, while drivers of those still serviceable sought to escape by driving cross-country. The desperation of those trapped in the long columns as they came under air attack was experienced at first hand by a number of Typhoon pilots who had been forced to abandon their aircraft.

One such individual was Flt Lt Cedric Henman of No 175 Sqn, who had bailed out of his crippled Typhoon near Falaise on the 14th. While hiding in woods, the undergrowth was sprayed with machine gun fire by the searching Germans. Eventually captured, he was tied to a tree and twice faced summary execution, only to be rescued in the nick of time by passing officers. Then during evacuation in a convoy he came under attack from his own unit! In front of his lorry was a Tiger tank, and when the first RPs were launched it surged forward in an attempt to evade the attack, flattening a staff car blocking its way, together with its occupants.

As Polish and Canadian forces sought to complete the closure on the 20th, the Germans sent a large number of panzers in to attack them in the Vimoutiers area. Wg Cdr Dring led 32 Typhoons from No 123 Wing against the armour, breaking up the concentrations with precision attacks under VCP control. Thirteen tanks were claimed destroyed and Dring was awarded an immediate DSO. Attacks on the many targets within the pocket continued until 25 August, by which time there was little left worthy of further effort. Once clear of the gap itself, there was still no respite for the retreating hordes as they were pounded again in bottlenecks at Orbec, Bernay and Broglie.

Subsequent British Army investigations showed again that the greatest damage had been done by the Typhoon's battery of four cannons, which had destroyed or disabled large numbers of vehicles, including the more lightly-armoured half-tracks and armoured personnel carriers, and inflicted damage on self-propelled artillery. Of the estimated total of more than 12,000 vehicles left in France by the Wehrmacht, a third were reckoned to have been destroyed by direct air attack, but many others had been abandoned due to the air action, either in panic or out of fuel.

In air support, identification of friendly and enemy forces is always a problem, and in the fluid situation around Falaise this was especially so. However, the most tragic incident did not occur on the battlefield. On 27 August 15 Typhoons of Nos 263

Two views of Flt Sgt Derek Tapson's No 197 Sqn Typhoon, MN925/OV-Z. The port aspect shows the aircraft fitted with long-range tanks, probably during the German retreat in late August/early September. The other view, in which MN925 is armed with 500-lb bombs, was taken later as the underwing stripes have been removed in accordance with instructions that were to be applied by 10 September 1944 (*D Tapson*)

and 266 Sqns, led by Wg Cdr Baldwin, located six ships heading southwest off Etretat. Suspecting that they were Allied, Baldwin queried their identity with Operations, but he was told to attack, as there was supposed to be no friendly shipping in the area. Despite querying the instruction a further three times, and describing the coloured signals fired, the order was still to attack. The Typhoons swept in and opened fire with cannon and rockets.

As Baldwin suspected, the four minesweepers and two trawlers were indeed British, and the onslaught was devastating. None of the ships escaped without damage or casualties, but the brunt of the attack was borne by three of the minesweepers, two of which were sunk and the third so badly damaged that it was eventually scrapped. Of the Royal Navy crews, 78 were killed and 149 wounded, although these figures include casualties caused by German shelling of the survivors.

This horrendous incident had been caused by the failure to communicate a change of course by the minesweeping flotilla to Naval HQ, who therefore did not expect any shipping in the area and ordered the attack. No attempt was made to lay blame at the RAF's door. Those who doubt the effectiveness of rockets should heed the words of the commander of the surviving minesweeper in his official report;

'It is felt that the fury and ferocity of concerted attacks by a number of Typhoon aircraft armed with rockets and cannons is an ordeal that has to be endured to be truly appreciated.'

As the remnants of 7th Army sought to flee across the Seine, all efforts by the Allied air forces were turned onto the river crossings and the last remaining bridges. Indeed, the last permanent bridge still standing over this river was destroyed by No 146 Wing Typhoons at this time. This was virtually the end of German resistance in France. The chase was now on, and over the next few weeks progress would be rapid as the front continually moved beyond the range of the fighter-bombers.

In late August the No 83 Group wings left their Normandy bases, following the advancing British 2nd Army on the right flank. The No 84 Group wings occupied bases behind the Canadian 1st Army on the left flank. By mid-September Antwerp was in British hands, and No 121 Wing moved to B70 Deurne, which had been the city's pre-war international airport. During this period the retreating Germans were continuously harried. For example, on 10 September Wg Cdr Bill Pitt-Brown led his old unit, No 174 Sqn, in a most effective attack on a pair of large barges that were attempting a crossing of the Westerschelde;

'We saw two large self-propelled barges leaving Terneuzen absolutely crammed to the gunnels with Huns. We waited until they were in the middle of the estuary, so that we would be at maximum distance from the flak on both banks, and then ran in towards them, parallel to the banks. We hit them with everything we had. It was a gin-clear day and you could see every shade of blue and brown in the estuary, but as they sank the water round the barges turned pink. The carnage was terrible.'

At the same time British forces were progressing through Holland, the US armies had pressed right across France to the German frontier, coming up against the Siegfried Line fortifications. The long German retreat was over for the time being, and soon the Typhoons would be fighting a rather different war.

BITTER WINTER, VICTORIOUS SPRING

In a desperate effort to keep the momentum of the advance going, a major airborne operation, *Market Garden*, was launched from England on 17 September. US paratroopers were dropped at Grave and Nijmegen and the British 1st Airborne Division at Arnhem with orders to capture bridges across the Maas, Waal and Rhine. Prior to the actual drop 107 Typhoon sorties were flown to neutralise gun positions, but 2nd TAF fighter-bombers were not allowed over the drop zones when the landings were taking place.

Simultaneously, No 30 Corps, spearheaded by the Guards Armoured Division, was to thrust northwards to link up with the airborne forces. Its advance was preceded by a rolling barrage, and 'cab-rank' Typhoons were on hand to lend aid as required. In fact they began by contributing a rolling barrage of their own – for the first hour new formations of No 124 Wing Typhoons arrived every five minutes to make successive strikes. After that more normal 'cab-rank' operations were resumed, aircraft operating within 200 yards of the advancing Guards.

Unfortunately, on the 18th the weather over the Typhoons' bases in Belgium much reduced the level of support they could give No 30 Corps, and on the 19th conditions were even worse. The Allied advance was slowed by determined opposition, and in Arnhem the 1st Airborne hung on to their positions against unexpectedly strong enemy forces. Grave and Nijmegen were taken, but after a hard and costly fight Arnhem was retained by the Germans. Because the operation had been controlled from England, and because the

Below and bottom
Shortly after No 124 Wing's arrival at B78 Eindhoven, Flg Off Ken Brain (who had destroyed four V1s before No 137 Sqn joined 2nd TAF) poses with his No 137 Sqn Typhoon, JP504/SF-R. Note the fire extinguisher hanging on the cannon – a necessity to have at hand when a Sabre engine was started. The aircraft behind SF-R is MN134/SF-S, which was used by various pilots to shoot down nine V1s (*K G Brain*)

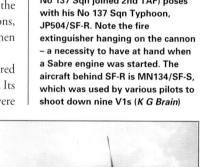

weather was frequently poor, there was little the Typhoons or other 2nd TAF aircraft could do to help the beleaguered 1st Airborne.

The advance had, however, made new bases available in Holland, and on 22 September No 124 Wing landed at Eindhoven (B78). Three days later No 143 Wing joined them there. By the end of the month No 121 Wing was settling in at Volkel (B80), further to the northeast.

With the Allied advance spread across northwest Europe, the units of Nos 83 and 84 Groups had at last parted company. While Nos 121, 124 and 143 Wings continued to give close support to the British 2nd Army as it advanced through Holland towards the German frontier, Nos 123 and 146 Wings were involved in attacking the bypassed garrisons, and targets around the Scheldt estuary and on Walcheren Island.

No 83 Group units, which were now frequently operating over German soil, were meeting Luftwaffe opposition once again. For example, the newly-arrived No 137 Sqn undertook an armed reconnaissance on 24 September and was attacked near Goch by 30 Fw 190s of I./JG 26. The unit lost its Norwegian CO, Sqn Ldr G Piltingsrud, who was shot down in flames. Two days later No 175 Sqn went out after barges near Tilberg, but in the Apeldoorn area of Holland the unit was attacked by '50+' Bf 109s from III./JG 4. One Typhoon was shot down and two more pilots fired off their rockets at the Messerschmitt fighters but without effect.

With the advance now at an end for the time being, the Typhoon ground attack units became more involved in interdiction work behind German lines, attacking everything that moved by day – particularly on the rail and road networks. These missions were not only aimed at disrupting normal military movements, but in particular to starve the V1 and V2 launching sites of their supplies of bombs and fuel. And with the V2 launchers being both mobile and easily camouflaged, 'interdiction' was the only effective counter to this deadly weapon, whose main target was now Antwerp. Indeed, some 40 to 50 V2s per day were being launched at the Belgian city. Among the sufferers there was No 146 Wing, which had moved to Antwerp/Deurne airfield on 2 October.

Groundcrew hard at work servicing MN716/F3-A of No 438 Sqn at Eindhoven in mid-October 1944 – the aircraft has some minor damage to the tail fin that needed to be repaired. The under-fuselage stripes appear to have been partly painted out to reduce conspicuity. This non-standard marking alteration was also seen on other No 143 Wing aircraft at this time (*Canadian Forces*)

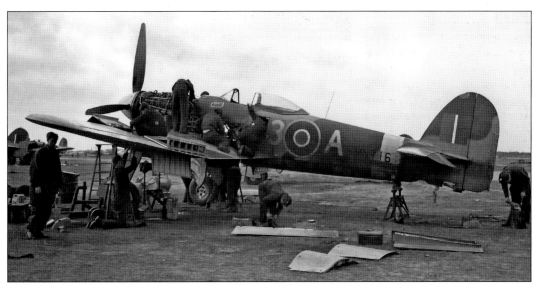

The worst incident involving the wing occurred on 25 October when a V2 killed five airmen and wounded six others.

'CLOAK AND DAGGER JOBS'

Information from 'intelligence sources' led to a series of 'set piece' attacks on German HQs, known as 'cloak and dagger jobs', in the autumn of 1944. On 24 October all five units of No 146 Wing undertook such an attack on Dordrecht, where the Dutch resistance reported that the HQ of the German 15th Army was situated in a park in the centre of the city.

The attack was planned for 1200 hrs, when it was hoped that the Staff Officers would be together at lunch. The mission was led by Grp Capt Gillam who, after a hail of rockets from eight Typhoons of No 266 Sqn, marked the target by placing two smoke bombs right in the middle of the park for the benefit of the following squadrons. In swept the first four aircraft from No 193 Sqn at low level, dropping eight 1000-lb bombs fused with 11-second delays. As they exploded, the rest of No 193 Sqn's Typhoons dive-bombed the target with 500 'pounders', followed in quick succession by Sqn Ldr Allan Smith leading No 197 Sqn at low level. Nos 257 and 263 Sqn added their ordnance to the devastation too. Finally, the whole area was thoroughly strafed with 20 mm cannon fire. An hour after take-off all the Typhoons were back. Not one had been lost.

The attack had seemed to be successful, each unit claiming that its rockets or bombs had hit the target area, but just how effective the strike had been was not known until 30 October. It was then learned from the Resistance that two generals, 17 staff officers, 36 other officers and more than 200 other ranks had been killed. This crippling loss would have a visible effect on the performance of the 15th Army for some time. An elaborate funeral was laid on for the victims, and No 146 Wing 'management' was keen to attack this event too, but it was restrained by orders from higher authority.

At the start of November the Canadians assaulted Walcheren Island, strongly supported by the No 84 Group Typhoons in their now familiar 'cab-rank' role. The aircraft flew many sorties against guns in pillboxes and larger fortifications, and it was for spectacular success during one of these missions that Sqn Ldr Rex Mulliner of No 183 Sqn was awarded an immediate DFC. It appears that rockets from the attack he led had been slotted through the embrasures of the fortification. In two days Walcheren and the Breskens 'Pocket', on the other side of the Scheldt estuary, were taken. This allowed the port of Antwerp to be opened at last, thus permitting a resumption of the Allied build-up in preparation for the advance into Germany.

Following these operations, Nos 123 and 146 Wings concentrated their attacks on strongpoints in the Arnhem and Nijmegen areas, but a more unusual target on 4 November was a 'human torpedo' factory at Utrecht. This was plastered with 38 500-lb bombs by Nos 193 and 197 Sqns, led by Grp Capt Gillam.

Sqn Ldr J R Beirnes, seen here taxiing out in his F3-B at B78 Eindhoven, finished his first tour in command of No 438 Sqn. He returned to lead the squadron again in April 1945, but was killed shortly after the war when he crashed in a later F3-B, SW393, following an engine failure (*A J Lord*)

Another 'cloak and dagger job' (or 'CD target' as they were now officially known) came No 146 Wing's way on 19 November when Grp Capt Gillam led the wing to the Gestapo HQ in Amsterdam, but this was aborted when ten-tenths cloud was encountered at 3000 ft.

The operation was laid on again one week later, and this time the weather co-operated. Again the attack was timed for the lunch-hour, with the dual purpose of safeguarding children in a nearby school and catching the Gestapo gathered together in their mess behind the HQ building. Gillam marked the target with phosphorus rockets, and there followed a coordinated attack by Nos 193, 257, 263 and 266 Sqns with rockets, 500 'pounders', 1000 'pounders' and incendiary bombs. Four aircraft from No 263 Sqn, led by Sqn Ldr Rutter, made a low-level attack. His No 2 was Flt Lt 'Ronnie' Sheward (a British Argentinian);

'Sqn Ldr Rutter was spot on in finding the target (models of this and the surrounding area had been studied) and we went straight in at "zero" feet, crashing the bombs (fused for an 11-second delay) through the front door and the front of the house. We then pulled up into the sun and were away. Wg Cdr Wells visited Amsterdam some months later, and he was hailed with delight by the Dutchmen who vividly described just what we had done to the hated Gestapo.'

Pinpoint attacks were not, however, the monopoly of No 146 Wing. On 4 November No 124 Wing took a break from army support and their regular interdiction route – 'the Munster milk run' – to strike two special targets. Wg Cdr North-Lewis led No 247 Sqn to Apeldoorn, where its target was the HQ of the Netherlands' Reich Commissioner, Arthur Seyss-Inquart. No 181 Sqn was assigned the second target, its pilots being told that their aim had to be particularly good on this occasion as they would be attacking a tower in the north wing of the Dutch Royal Family's summer palace. This was being used by the SS as an HQ, while the rest of the building was believed to still be occupied by members of the Royal Family. The attack, which proved to be successful, was made parallel to the main building so that any overshoots would fall harmlessly into an open area beyond the wing.

On 18 November the Canadians of No 143 Wing were given yet another bridge to deal with, but this one would be remembered by the pilots on the mission for its stubbornness. The bridge was at Hilfarth, and it was a vital crossing point over which the Germans brought supplies for their forward troops. The target was attacked by all three squadrons, several times, but despite the 'rain' of 1000-lb bombs it remained standing. As the third attack commenced a horse-drawn transport was seen, its driver flailing his whip in an effort to get off the bridge before the bombs fell. An anonymous voice came over the R/T, 'Stay on the bridge you silly bugger – it's the safest place to be!'

WINTER ARRIVES

As the weather worsened, and the wings settled down to see the winter

Wg Cdr 'Kit' North-Lewis led No 124 Wing into B78 Eindhoven on 22 September 1944 in his first KN-L, MP189. He flew this aircraft until it was replaced by RB208, which remained his mount until the end of his tour during the Rhine crossings (*C D North-Lewis*)

through at the more permanent airfields at which they were now based, one squadron at a time from each group was sent to APCs at Warmwell and Fairwood Common. This not only allowed the pilots to hone their bombing and rocket-firing skills without the distraction of flak and fighters, it also provided a welcome break from the ceaseless round of operations and the inhospitable accommodation of the frontline airfields.

The winter of 1944-45 proved to be a hard one, with flying being considerably reduced by fog, snow and generally inclement conditions. Groundcrews had to work in almost intolerable circumstances in the open, as few airfields boasted hangars after German demolitions and earlier Allied attacks. Interdiction and attacks on strongpoints continued to be the main duties of the Typhoons during early December, and at this time several squadrons were attacked on a number of occasions by American fighters, which frequently mistook the aircraft for Fw 190s. Indeed, at least four Typhoons would be shot down in error by their Allies in this way before the winter was over.

After suffering devastating attacks on their HQs, it seems the Germans had learnt some lessons – especially the 15th Army, whose HQ had been hit again on 28 November by No 123 Wing. On 8 December this HQ was again the target at a new location in woods near Amersfoort, which was defended by multi-barrelled flak guns. All four squadrons from No 123 Wing were to take part. Twelve aircraft from each unit had been called for, but No 198 Sqn could only muster eight. As the CO's aircraft went unserviceable at the last minute, they were led by Flt Lt Denis Sweeting, who recalled;

'As we got airborne we could hear the first squadron preparing to attack. "Look at that flak" somebody called, which seemed a bit chilling. While climbing to 4000 ft my No 4 called to say he was returning to base with engine problems. We saw him turn around and go back. A minute or so later my No 2 called up to say he had seen him crash-land into a flooded field. I called Gilze (the unit's B77 base) and gave them the position. I thought what a doom-laden proposition this was becoming. Just then a voice on the radio called the No 183 Sqn leader saying "'Blue Four' is on fire".

'We soldiered on towards the target and someone reported he had been hit. As we crossed the Neder Rhein No 609 Sqn called that they were going down. We skirted the flak positions around the town of Amersfoort and could see the target from the rising columns of smoke. To get in and out quickly, I had arranged that we would go down in pairs, line abreast, 50 yards apart, hoping this would make it more difficult for the flak gunners. I called to the unit to prepare for the attack as the target was coming up on the port side. Lt Pierre Brisdoux formed up close on my starboard side. Waving to him to get further away, I then called up "Going down".

There were many days in the winter of 1944/45 when operational flying was just not possible due either to fog or snow. Here, a No 266 Sqn pilot stands beside his frozen Typhoon at B70 Deurne. The canvas shroud hanging over the nose of the Typhoon was designed to keep the engine at a temperature at which it could still be started – the canvas chimney hides a paraffin heater. No 266 Sqn was at the time the only RP-equipped squadron in No 146 Wing, and this aircraft is fitted with four RPs and two 44-gallon long-range tanks (*via J Miller*)

'As we dived into range of the light flak guns, they started a furious barrage. There was a violent explosion and a flash of fire on my starboard side. I turned my head just in time to see Pierre's aircraft rolling away in a ball of fire. I turned back to my gunsight, concentrating on lining up on one of the buildings. Tracers of various colours and white puffs were all around. I laid off deflection for the wind direction, which was conveniently shown by the smoke coming from the buildings. At 800 yards I fired the

salvo and pulled upwards, swinging the aircraft from side to side. At 5000 ft I looked down at the target area, which was a mass of flames with smoke rising to 500 ft. I could not see my No 3 (Flg Off M A Milich) and called the other section climbing behind to ask if they could. "'Black Three' crashed in flames on the target", I was told.

'We returned to Gilze in silence. As we taxied along to the squadron dispersal area Flying Control asked when the rest of "Baltic Black" section would be landing. I grimly replied that they wouldn't.'

Nine days later, taking advantage of the appalling weather that had grounded the Allied fighter-bombers, the Germans launched their Ardennes offensive. It was not until 24 December that the skies cleared sufficiently for the air forces to play a major part in slowing down the German advance. And just as the Allied aircraft managed to get back into the air, so the Luftwaffe made a concerted effort to provide support for the Wehrmacht. The end result was Typhoon pilots running into more German fighters than they had seen for many weeks.

No 440 Sqn lost an aircraft to the ever present flak threat during the morning, but on the unit's second strike mission of the day a single Fw 190 dived on Flg Offs W T Dunkeld and D H Cumming as they provided top cover for six other Typhoons over the Malmedy area and shot both of the Canadians down. The lone Focke-Wulf was in turn promptly despatched by a Tempest of No 274 Sqn, which had been flying above the Typhoons in the hands of ace Sqn Ldr E D Mackie.

Although the Typhoons did their best to provide support wherever it was needed, the situation was confused and the lines fluid. In an attempt to overcome these difficulties Wg Cdr 'Kit' North-Lewis despatched No 181 Sqn's Flt Lt L P Boucher to Dinant with a radio car and orders to get the wing in on the German armour. On Boxing Day, when the weather had improved, the wing was summoned

Flt Lt Denis Sweeting (centre, wearing a cap), who was No 198 Sqn's 'A' Flight commander, poses in front his Typhoon – MN951/TP-A *The Uninvited* – with some of his pilots at B53 Merville. The aircraft's name was inspired by the Hollywood film of that title, and it reflected what Denis thought might be the German view of the Typhoon (*D Sweeting*)

Although not the best quality photograph, this shot is well worth inclusion for it features Flg Off Roy Heath's uniquely marked Typhoon PD600/DP-C, named *LITTLE RAE*, at B70 Deurne in late 1944. Heath was one of the few US citizens to fly Typhoons. The aircraft is armed with two 500-lb bombs that have been fitted with the long tails. The latter gave the ordnance better dropping characteristics, and they were used whenever available (*B Lenson*)

to deal with a German thrust towards the nearby bridge over the Meuse. Boucher was in the radio car alongside the brigadier's divisional HQ;

'At what I judged to be the crucial moment I called for the smoke markers, and I was very relieved when "Kit" reported that he could see the enemy tanks and was going in to attack.'

North-Lewis had another seven Typhoons of No 181 Sqn with him, and they made repeated low-level attacks with RPs and cannon fire, despite fierce flak that riddled the wing leader's aircraft. With the formation reforming, Flt Lt Dennis Luke made a final cannon attack to use up the last of his ammunition. As the lone Typhoon swept in, the German commander emerged from the turret of his tank, perhaps believing that the storm had passed. 'Lew' Boucher continues;

'We got a running commentary from the forward troops, and the brigadier was jumping up and down with excitement as it became apparent that the attack was a success. Before returning to Eindhoven I had a look at the site of the attack. There were several burned out tanks (four, and two half-tracks, were claimed), and one, which appeared to be the lead tank, was standing seemingly undamaged in the middle of the field. I was puzzled by this. The tank's hatch was open, so I climbed up to look inside. The tank commander's body was still in it, and his head had obviously been smashed by a cannon shell which had ricocheted off the edge of the hatch opening.'

Luftwaffe fighters were again encountered on 29 December. The first were seen by No 168 Sqn, which went out at full unit strength on an armed reconnaissance mission over the Munster-Rheine area. Here, a mixed force of 12 Bf 109s and Fw 190s were encountered, and the latter managed to shoot down both of No 168 Sqn's flight commanders, Flt Lts E Gibbons and R F Plant. In return, seven pilots poured fire into a single unfortunate Focke-Wulf which spun down, the pilot bailing out. That same day Fw 190s also shot down a No 439 Sqn Typhoon near Coesfeld, although a Bf 109 and an Fw 190 were claimed destroyed in return by Flg Off R H Laurence. On 31 December German fighters similarly dealt with a No 247 Sqn aircraft near Steinhuder Lake, although the unit was able to even the score.

Never had the 2nd TAF lost so many Typhoons (at least ten) in aerial combat in a single month, and when added to 37 other operational losses

Above and top
On 5 December 1944, Dutchman Flg Off 'Frickie' Wiersum of No 247 Sqn borrowed his commanding officer's Typhoon, MP126/ZY-Y. Hit by flak, Wiersum was forced to make a wheels-up landing near Bocholt and was taken prisoner. His captors were obviously so impressed by the artwork on Sqn Ldr 'Stapme' Stapleton's Typhoon that they took this photograph of it! (*via J Rajlich*)

in the same nine-day period – one to a USAAF P-47, but mostly to flak – the Ardennes fighting had proved expensive to the close support force.

BODENPLATTE

The Luftwaffe's last major input in the Ardennes fighting occurred shortly after dawn on 1 January 1945 when a surprise attack on Allied airfields in the area was launched under the codename Operation *Bodenplatte* ('Baseplate'). Generally, this proved to be a costly exercise for the Germans, who lost more manned fighters during the attack than the mostly unmanned aircraft they managed to destroy on the ground. The most successful of all the German strikes was that made by JG 3 on Eindhoven airfield. This was home to the eight Typhoon squadrons of Nos 124 and 143 Wings, as well as No 39 (Reconnaissance) Wing's three Spitfire reconnaissance units, No 83 Group's Communications Squadron and No 403 RSU.

No 143 Wing had been the first to send aircraft aloft on this date, with four Typhoons of No 439 Sqn taking off on a weather reconnaissance to St Vith, followed by six fighters from No 168 Sqn who departed on an armed reconnaissance over the Frith-Prum area a short while later. The latter aircraft were passed by six incoming Bf 109s just minutes after take-off. One of the Messerschmitts attempted to attack the British aircraft, but it was shot at and claimed damaged for its trouble. A No 137 Sqn formation was also airborne, and it missed the holocaust that was about to come. As the Messerschmitts and Focke-Wulfs reached Eindhoven, at 0920 hrs, they found another No 168 Sqn aircraft just getting airborne for an 'air test' in the hands of Flt Lt H P Gibbons. He managed to swing his Typhoon round to meet the attackers, and was seen to blow the tail off an Fw 190 before succumbing to the fire of three Bf 109s.

Next on the runway after Gibbons were eight bombed-up Typhoons of No 438 Sqn, lined up in pairs and led by their new CO, Flt Lt Pete Wilson. Behind them, eight more bombers from No 440 Sqn awaited their turn to take-off. The first pair from the former unit had actually started to accelerate along the runway when the JG 3 aircraft swept in. The No 438 Sqn CO was mortally wounded, while the second aircraft was shot down in flames, killing Flg Off R W Keller. Wilson pulled off the runway and climbed out of his riddled Typhoon, but he died within minutes from a stomach wound. Strapped into one of the other No 438 Sqn aircraft was Plt Off Andy Lord, who recalled;

'The first wave of Me 109s and Fw 190s surged on the deck from the opposite end of the runway, all guns firing. Our first two guys never had a chance. Then a second wave, a third, eventually well over 50 enemy fighters bombed and strafed the airfield. There were so many that two of them collided.

'I saw the right wing of "Red 3" fold straight up. I looked to the left and saw that my wing was on fire –

Touching down at B78 Eindhoven, a No 168 Sqn Typhoon returns from an 'armed recce' or possibly an escort to other No 143 Wing (bomber) squadrons. This unit tended to operate older three-bladed propeller Typhoons, as the three bomber squadrons on the same wing had priority for the four-bladed aircraft (because of their improved take-off performance) (*A J Cranston*)

same on the right. I yanked my helmet off, undid all my straps and jumped to the ground. In normal times one should at least break a leg jumping from this height. I ran about 50 ft and fell flat behind a two-foot high pile of scraps. The Bofors were blasting away with some success. Smoke was billowing from burning aircraft, both ours and theirs, bombs exploding and enemy aeroplanes crashing on the field. There were also parachutes drifting down and ammo from our kites exploding. It was a real madhouse.'

Other pilots leapt from their cockpits and sought cover as their Typhoons burst into flames, two more of them suffering wounds. Plt Off R A Watson of No 440 Sqn managed to open fire from the ground, claiming hits on one Focke-Wulf before his own fighter was set on fire.

No 124 Wing was also hit, and despite No 137 Sqn's Flt Sgt L A V Burrows being killed as he was taxiing to dispersal, its losses were much lighter than those suffered by the Canadian wing. No 39 (Reconnaissance) Wing lost a dozen more aircraft, including three elderly Mustang Is (which were about to be replaced by Spitfires FR XIVs), and many others were damaged. Of the 125+ Typhoons at Eindhoven (including those under repair at the RSU) 60 were hit, with 17 being destroyed outright, nine badly damaged but never repaired, ten badly damaged but repaired off-unit and 24 damaged but repaired locally.

In the aftermath of the destruction at Eindhoven it was considered of paramount importance to let the Luftwaffe know that the Typhoons were still in business, so on missions flown later in the day the pilots were for once encouraged to chatter on the R/T and to use all the call-signs of the wing for the benefit of the German listening service.

The Typhoons had the last word when the four No 439 Sqn pilots returning from their weather reconnaissance spotted 15 Fw 190s

It seems that Wg Cdr Frank Grant, CO of No 143 Wing, was extremely lucky to escape injury when his Typhoon (RB205/FGG) was hit by flak splinters on 24 December 1944. Grant remained leader of the wing until it was disbanded in August 1945. RB205 was not so fortunate, however, for it was destroyed during the Luftwaffe's New Year's Day raid whilst with an RSU at Eindhoven (via G MacDonald)

The aftermath of Operation *Bodenplatte* at Eindhoven – No 137 Sqn Typhoon JR260/SF-Z, in which Flt Sgt Lance Burrows was fatally wounded, shares the apron with the remains of an Anson. The latter was possibly Wg Cdr Erik Haabjorn's aircraft that he had flown in from the Central Fighter Establishment at Tangmere (Jack Snape)

From 3 January 1945, 2nd TAF markings changed. Spinners were painted black, rear fuselage bands and any remaining D-Day stripes painted over and all roundels had narrow white rings and yellow outer rings (National Marking III, aka 'Type C1'). The marking changes were completed by 5 February. This No 440 Sqn Typhoon, PD601/I8-X, seen in its dispersal at Eindhoven some time between 3 and 21 January (when it was lost on operations), has already had the changes implemented (*H Hardy*)

east of Helmond running for home. Attacking these, in company with two Spitfires, the Canadian pilots claimed four shot down, two each by Flg Offs R H Laurence and A H Fraser, although Flg Off S Angelini was killed in return. This was the second, and last, time that Bob Laurence had claimed two victories in a single combat, and he was awarded an immediate DFC.

Other Luftwaffe fighters attacked USAAF airstrip A84 at Asche, where Nos 164 and 183 Sqns had just arrived on detachment from No 123 Wing. Already scrambled to meet the incoming Germans, USAAF P-51s mistook the Typhoons for the enemy, shooting down No 183 Sqn's Flg Off D Webber as he approached the airfield with the wheels of his fighter down – the pilot was killed. The rest landed safely, but were then subjected to the Germans' strafe, which damaged two No 164 Sqn Typhoons. No 146 Wing's airfield at Antwerp/Deurne was also attacked, but ineffectually, as only a single No 266 Sqn Typhoon and two of No 257 Sqn's aircraft suffered damage. Few of the German fighters that had been assigned Volkel as a target managed to make attacks, and the Typhoon squadrons there escaped without loss or damage.

Within a few days the units that had suffered most were back at full strength, their pilots having been ferried to the UK to pick up new Typhoons from No 83 Group Support Unit (GSU), but with the end of the German offensive and a resumption of the poor weather, January proved to be a month of little action. On the 9th No 124 Wing moved into a newly built airfield at Helmond (B86), which was closer to the scene of operations. Another specially constructed base was nearing completion further to the north at Mill, but it would not be occupied by No 146 Wing until the following month.

The start of February saw some improvement in the weather, and on the 8th the British and Canadian armies launched Operation *Veritable* as they moved up to the Rhine prior to the crossing of this major obstacle and then deployment into Germany proper. 'Cab-rank' operations to provide direct support became the order of the day once again, with the next week bringing the largest haul of tanks, armoured vehicles and other motor transport destroyed since the Falaise operations of the previous August.

PILOT SHORTAGE

Casualties among pilots since the D-Day invasion had been such that by this time a constant flow of suitably experienced replacements was becoming difficult to maintain. Volunteers from the Spitfire squadrons had been called for, but the reputation of the Typhoon units as virtual suicide squads (and who would want to give up a Spitfire for Hawker's workhorse) brought a disappointing, but predictable, response – almost nil! There is no doubt that casualties had been very heavy, and by mid-February had included 20 squadron commanders and wing leaders since D-Day, as well as large numbers of experienced flight commanders.

Experience and flying skill were of some advantage when deadly flak was the main enemy, but chance and luck seemed to count for more. To keep the other squadrons at full strength, and to allow the posting of tour-expired pilots to instructor jobs at the newly-formed Typhoon OTUs, three of the five wings each shed a squadron. At the end of February No 168 Sqn was the first to be disbanded, followed by No 257 Sqn the next month and No 174 Sqn at the beginning of April.

Typhoons were to enjoy some unexpected successes against the new Luftwaffe jets before Operation *Veritable* was over. On 14 February 55 Me 262 fighter-bombers were sent out to attack British forces advancing near Kleve. Two flashed past aircraft of No 184 Sqn near Arnhem, allowing South African Air Force pilot Capt A F Green to get in a quick burst and claim the jet as having been damaged. That same morning four No 439 Sqn pilots saw two jets from 5./KG(J) 51 below them heading west. Diving to attack, Flt Lt Lyal Shaver hit one, which blew up at once, while Flg Off Hugh Fraser obtained hits on the second, which was later confirmed as destroyed.

By early March the Germans were in full retreat to the Rhine, but once the river was reached the line again became static, and attacks on interdiction targets were resumed. These were normally flown in formations of six or eight, although one or two 'spares' would be taken along in case of technical failure, turning back at the 'bomb line' if not required. The remainder then pressed on in 'loose pairs', the leader searching for targets while under the protection of the rest of his formation. Railway targets in particular were avidly sought, but trains could be a deadly trap even for the wary, as Flg Off Ian Ladely of No 182 Sqn recalled;

'Just two went down on this train, Bill Cuthbertson and Jack Taylor, while the rest of us gave top cover. There was a call from Jack – "I've been hit" – and as Bill circled to watch him force-land, he too was hit. Both of them belly-landed okay, and they were seen to climb out of their cockpits. We then saw that the train had been parked alongside the main line, with several flak-cars, and with flak positions hidden in the woods all around.'

The unfortunate WO Cuthbertson and Flt J H Taylor were captured by the *Volksturm* and shot, in accordance with orders that the part-time soldiers had to execute all 'terror-*flieger*' captured deep in German territory. The perpetrators of this crime were hunted down immediately after the war, with one being shot while trying to escape and the rest tried and sentenced to death. 2nd TAF pilots were well aware of the dangers that they faced if they found themselves behind enemy lines. Several were known to have been murdered in cold-blood in Normandy, and more would meet this fate on German soil. Pilots were armed with revolvers, but some carried additional weapons such as lethal knives. WO Bob Merlin, who returned to 'ops' with No 175 Sqn after his long sojourn in enemy territory (see page 47), went one step further by carrying a Sten gun in his cockpit! Others took the view that a handgun was of little use, and an unnecessary provocation.

As preparations were made for a massive crossing of the Rhine by both ground and airborne forces, a number of 'CD' targets were dealt with by the Typhoons. On 18 March No 146 Wing attacked the HQ of General Johannes Blaskowitz, who had taken over Army Group H from General Kurt Student. The target was hit hard, and 62 members of Blaskowitz's staff were killed. Three days later, five squadrons of No 84 Group Typhoons supported by three of Spitfires attacked the camouflaged village of Zwolle, which was being used as a paratroop depot. The aircraft also attacked the HQ of the German 25th Army – a hotel at Bussum, in Holland. The general in command of the 25th had left the previous day, but vital staff were killed and documents destroyed nevertheless.

During 20 and 21 March No 121 Wing moved forward to B100 at Goch, which was the first British airfield on German soil, while No 123 Wing moved to B91 at Kluis, in Holland. No 143 Wing would also transfer to B100 within a few days.

On the 23rd Wg Cdr Keep led No 121 Wing in sustained attacks on flak positions in the area selected for the airborne operations across the Rhine. The next day, as the crossings took place, spearheaded by a massive airborne force of paratroops and glider-borne infantry, it was maximum effort for all the Typhoon wings, with the first sorties taking place shortly after dawn. Some operated on 'cab-rank' patrols, while others were allocated the flak suppression role. The latter was not too popular with the pilots, for it involved a pair of Typhoons acting as bait while the following pair watched for gun flashes to reveal the flak positions, thus allowing them to carry out their attack. Most of the wings launched sections of four aircraft every 15 minutes between 1000 hrs and 1600 hrs, No 245 Sqn, to quote just one example, flying 52 sorties during the course of the day.

The landings proved a total success, and the Typhoons had certainly played their part once again. Of the 440 para-dropping and glider-towing aircraft employed

Artwork on Typhoons during 2nd TAF service was at best restrained, except for this extraordinary sharksmouth marking applied to MP197/MR-U of No 245 Sqn. Thought to have been decorated in this style in late 1944 or early 1945, MR-U was sometimes flown by Canadian pilot Flt Lt H T Mossip, who had an impressive train-busting record from his earlier tour with No 1 Sqn. Mossip was killed on 7 March 1945 after colliding with high tension cables during a ground attack. MR-U was often flown by No 245 Sqn's CO, Sqn Ldr Tony Zweigbergk, who is seen here on the right admiring the fearsome artwork with his 'B' Flight commander, Flt Lt Geoff Murphy (*G Murphy*)

Flt Lt Geoff Murphy's own Typhoon, MR-Z, also featured artwork. It was called *Zephyr Breezes* after 'Zed for Breezes' in the spoof phonetic alphabet that contained such gems as 'Jay for Oranges' and 'Pee for Cake' (*G Murphy*)

by the RAF, only six were shot down by flak. Despite the dangerous task they had undertaken, losses among the Typhoons had been relatively low, and those pilots who were hit managed, in the main, to bail out or force-land in Allied territory. Two exceptions were No 124 Wing's 'Winco Ops', 'Kit' North-Lewis (see Chapter 3), and No 247 Sqn's Flg Off Cliff Monk. The latter crash-landed in enemy territory and jumped into a trench already occcupied by two German soldiers, who surrendered when he brandished his pistol. They were followed by 28 more, eager to find a British officer to take them into captivity, which he did!

The CO of No 247 Sqn at the time was Sqn Ldr Jim Bryant, who had been one of the original members of No 181 Sqn and had returned to 'ops' after a four-month spell instructing at No 83 GSU. He remembers this period, and particularly 24-25 March (when support for the bridgehead across the Rhine continued), as being the most dangerous for Typhoon pilots;

Hit by groundfire on 24 March 1945 during an anti-flak patrol near Isselburg in support of the Rhine crossing, Flt Lt H G Pattison lost all hydraulic systems in his RB202/XM-K of No 182 Sqn. Opting for B78 Eindhoven, where better facilities were available than at his base (B86 Helmond), Pattison made a wheels-up landing and his aircraft is seen being recovered from the 'crash-strip'. Behind it are two more damaged Typhoons, including MN777/I8-J of No 440 Sqn that had crash-landed after a tyre burst on take-off earlier that same day (*Canadian Forces*)

'I can think of no other time when so many Typhoons were written off by anti-aircraft fire in such a short period. Those gunners were making a last ditch stand for the Third Reich, and we were equally determined that our airborne troops should encounter as little opposition as possible.

'On one of these sorties, in which we operated as pairs, my No 2 was "Pop" Arnold, some 400 yards to starboard, and we were flying at 1500 ft looking for guns near Dingden. Three were spotted, each in the corners of a field. My first pair of rockets knocked one out, and as I started to climb away a shell from another hit my port wing and removed a large chunk from the tip to the roundel. This immediately threw the aircraft on its back at 200 ft, leaving me heading straight for a forest. It took all my strength, using both hands on the stick, to right the aircraft.

'I was travelling south at the time with an airspeed of 350 mph when I was hit. Unable at this speed to make a right hand turn onto a westerly course, I throttled back and was obliged to make a 270-degree climbing turn to port to head back towards the Rhine. All the guns in the area were now firing at me, and I could feel the odd dull thud as bullets hit the fuselage behind me. Climbing slowly, I crossed the Rhine at about 2000 ft and found that at 210 mph the port wing stalled in an incipient flick roll. At 220 mph a jagged piece of metal skin on the edge of the missing part of the wing curled back and threatened to foul the aileron, the far end of which was sticking out on its own, with only the rear spar in front of it.

'Flying in this restricted speed range still required both hands to prevent the aircraft from rolling – landing was clearly out of the question. On approaching base (Helmond), when at 5000 ft, I advised Ground Control of my intention to bail out south of the airfield. Heading for open country, I pulled out the R/T plug, undid my safety straps, jettisoned the hood and held back pressure on the stick as I set elevator trim fully forward. On releasing the stick I flew out of the cockpit as the aircraft plunged down and to port to bury itself in a swamp.'

FINAL RECKONING

Following the Rhine crossing, British and Canadian forces were once more in hot pursuit, as their armoured columns cut deep into north and northwest Germany. During the first week of April No 123 Wing aided in the final, and long-delayed, liberation of the shattered remains of Arnhem. A mixture of close support and interdiction sorties were flown during the first part of the month, with one such operation resulting in the last Typhoon losses to the Luftwaffe. These occurred on 4 April, when 12 Bf 109s 'jumped' Typhoons of No 438 Sqn and shot down WO W J Kinsella and Flt Lt E J McAlpine, which were providing top cover for the rest of the unit – both men perished.

Attacks were also made against remaining Luftwaffe airfields, where a considerable number of aircraft were claimed destroyed. Harbours and waterways were targeted too, as some German elements strove to escape across the Baltic to Norway.

Further moves were made to airfields deeper in Germany, and although the new residents were rarely molested, on 20 April six Bf 109s and three Fw 190s strafed B150 at Fassberg, where one or two Typhoons of Nos 121 and newly arrived 143 Wings were damaged.

On 26 April, just as a section of four No 263 Sqn Typhoons were breaking away from an RP attack on a train in Niebull station, they were 'jumped' by two Me 262s. One of the jets made a pass at formation leader Plt Off D E Morgan, who had been hit by flak and was attempting a forced landing, but it overshot. Immediately Morgan's No 2, WO H Barrie, gave it a long burst, which was followed by attacks from the other two Typhoons. The jet rolled onto its back, flames pouring from the centre section, and dived into the ground from 3000 ft. It was the last German fighter to fall to the Typhoon's guns.

Flg Off 'Johnny' Rook of No 197 Sqn taxies out at B89 Mill in his RB251/OV-G *Brenda IX*. It carries two long-tailed 500-lb bombs (*J C Rook*)

Operations continued into early May, with sustained attacks on communications, airfields, the Baltic ports and coastal shipping. Amongst a number of floatplanes and flying boats destroyed at this time was a huge six-engined Blohm und Voss Bv 222, claimed by No 175 Sqn at a flying boat base on 2 May. A little over a week earlier, on 23 April, No 439 Sqn pilots had also made a claim for a Bv 222 destroyed which they had happened upon, moored and partly hidden, on the Schaal See. It was not known until after the war (and by historians until recently) that the Canadians had in fact badly damaged the sole prototype Bv 238, an even larger six-engined flying boat.

Great masses of motor transport packed the roads of northwest Germany, and great execution was done amongst these and locomotives. In the first days of May shipping in the Baltic became a priority target. Fleeing from the northern German ports and heading for Denmark or Norway, these vessels came in all shapes and sizes, even sailing ships, and were thought to be carrying German leaders and SS troops intent on carrying on the war.

Two of the largest vessels sunk were the 21,000-ton *Deutschland* and the 27,500-ton *Cap Arcona*, both passenger liners, but unfortunately the latter did not harbour the expected SS. The *Cap Arcona* and the *Thielbek*, a much smaller freighter moored nearby, were floating prison ships in which 4500 and 2800 concentration camp inmates, respectively, had been incarcerated for some days. This fact was not known to RAF Intelligence, so Nos 83 and 84 Groups laid on shipping attacks. Both vessels were hit by an extremely accurate RP attack pressed home by an unsuspecting No 198 Sqn, and approximately 6900 of their wretched cargo perished, along with 100 of their SS guards. The *Deutschland* had been earmarked as a hospital ship and had a small medical team on board, but the necessary Red Crosses were limited to a single example on one of the funnels. It was sunk following rocket attacks by Nos 184 and 263 Sqns and dive-bombing by No 197 Sqn.

Then suddenly it was over. On the evening of 4 May 1945 all German armies in Holland, Denmark and northwest Germany surrendered, prior to the complete cessation of hostilities in Europe three days later.

In the first days of peace groundcrew work on MN299/HH-H, a war-weary Typhoon that had survived more than a year of operations with Nos 247, 245, 184 and finally 175 Sqns. Like many others, the aircraft would be flown back to No 83 Group Disbandment Centre at Lasham, in Hampshire, and scrapped (*W J Lincoln*)

In both Nos 83 and 84 Groups, the Typhoons had provided the backbone of the close support force, backed by larger numbers of Spitfire fighter-bombers, which carried a smaller bomb-load and doubled as fighters. Thousands of vehicles of all kinds had been destroyed since 6 June by the two groups, together with many locomotives and rolling stock, guns, HQs, barges and other shipping. Of over 220,000 rocket projectiles launched, virtually all had been delivered by Typhoons, as had a substantial proportion of the bomb tonnage dropped. Although operating specifically in the close-support role, the Typhoons had been able to claim the destruction of 50 German aircraft in the air during this period, and nearly as many again on the ground. More than 500 Typhoons had been lost on operations since the invasion – less than 50 of them to hostile aircraft – while many more had been damaged.

For the British 2nd and Canadian 1st Armies in Europe, the Typhoon had been the very epitome of close-support in Europe during the past ten months. Accurate, swift-responding and hard-hitting, it had been the scourge of the Wehrmacht's mobile forces and command organisation whenever weather allowed uninterrupted operations. Too specialised for a peacetime air force, and with increasing numbers of its successor, the Tempest, becoming available, its days were numbered post-VE Day.

After some hectic celebrations, the Typhoon units settled down to a routine of flying training, interspersed with flag-waving formation flights. However, by the end of May No 164 Sqn had gone, equipping with Spitfires in the UK, and the following month No 183 Sqn followed suit. At the end of July No 266 Sqn disbanded, and August brought a rash of departures, including the whole of the Canadian Wing. The Typhoons were flown back to Dunsfold or Lasham, where the GSUs had become Nos 83 and 84 Group Disbandment Centres. War-weary Typhoons were scrapped on the spot, but more serviceable examples were flown to Nos 5, 20 or 51 MUs, where they were stored. No 247 Sqn joined No 183 at Chilbolton to begin conversion to the Tempest II, but still had enough Typhoons to be the sole representative of the rapidly disappearing breed to take part in the massive Battle of Britain flypast over London on 15 September 1945. By the end of September the last of the Typhoon units in Germany had disbanded. The Typhoon Wings had served their purpose most admirably – and gone!

APPENDICES

APPENDIX 1

TYPHOON WINGS (INCLUDING SECTORS AND AIRFIELDS)

Listed and detailed below are the Sectors, Wings and Airfields that comprised the operational structure and provided support for the Typhoon squadrons of the TAF and the 2nd TAF between the formation of the former in June 1943 and VE Day, 8 May 1945. The wings listed below, with numbers between 16 and 22, were, due to limited communications between the Group Control Centres and the Airfields, formed to provide operational control for (initially) two 'Airfields'. Their titles were changed to 'Sector' on 12 May 1944. However, the Sectors in Nos 83 and 84 Group proved unwieldy, and they were disbanded on 12 July 1944.

The Airfields/Wings numbered between 121 and 146 were formally titled 'Airfield Headquarters', changing to 'Wing Headquarters' when the original 2nd TAF Wings became Sectors. Also included in some of the titles were role designations – e.g. 'Fighter', 'Rocket Projectile', 'Bomber' – but these tended to be omitted in time.

Dates in brackets indicate the presence of a unit or individual on formation or, in the case of '(May 45)', continuation after VE Day. By late 1944 the title 'wing commander flying' had been replaced by 'wing commander operations'. Dates of absence from the wing due to attendance at APCs refer to the air element of the unit only.

No 16 (Mobile) Wing/Sector
Formed within No 83 Group on 5 July 1943 at New Romney to administer and control Nos 121 and 124 Airfields. Disbanded 20 April 1944, its Airfields being transferred to the control of No 22 Sector.

Bases

New Romney	5/7/43
Lydd	18/8/43
Westhampnett	9/10/43
Hurn	1/4/44

Commanding Officers

Wg Cdr D E Gillam DSO DFC** AFC	7/43
Wg Cdr T Morice MC	7/43 to 8/43
Grp Capt H de C A Woodhouse DFC AFC	8/43 to 4/44

No 20 (Fighter) Wing/Sector
Formed within No 84 Group in November 1943 at Hornchurch to administer and control Nos 135 and 136 Airfields. Took over No 123 Airfield on 10 March 1944 and No 146 Airfield on 20 April 1944. Disbanded 12 July 1944.

Hornchurch	11/43
Thorney Island	9/4/44

Commanding Officers

Grp Capt C J StJ Beamish DFC	11/43 to 2/44
Grp Capt D E Gillam DSO DFC* AFC	3/44 to 7/44

No 22 (RCAF) (Fighter) Wing/Sector
Formed within No 83 Group on 9 January 1944 at Ayr to administer and control No 143 Airfield. Took over No 144 Airfield at Digby on 14 February 1944, moving there a week later. When No 16 Sector disbanded, No 22 Sector took over Nos 121 and 124 Airfields on 16 April 1944. Disbanded 12 July 1944.

Ayr	9/1/44
Digby	21/2/44
Hurn	17/3/44
Westhampnett	26/3/44
Hurn	16/4/44
In transit	6/6/44
B5	16/6/44

Commanding Officer

Grp Capt P Y Davoud DSO DFC	9/7/44

The following units were originally formed with the title 'Airfield' but this was changed to 'Wing' on 12 May 1944.

No 121 Airfield/Wing
Formed on 22 February 1943 at Wrexham to take part in Exercise *Spartan*, during which it was based at Middle Wallop and Membury. After a spell at Fairlop, the Airfield moved to Selsey at the end of May and was based there when the TAF was formed.

Selsey	(6/43)
Lydd	1/7/43
Westhampnett	10/10/43
Holmsley South	1/4/44
B5	17/6/44
B24	27/8/44
B42	1/9/44
B50	3/9/44
B70	16/9/44
B80	28/9/44
B100	21/3/45
B110	11/4/45
B150	16/4/45

Commanding Officers

Wg Cdr (later Grp Capt) C S Morice DSO MC	(6/43) to 12/44
Grp Capt C G Jones DSO DFC	12/44 to 4/45
Grp Capt R P R Powell DFC*	12/45 to (5/45)

Wing Commanders Flying

Wg Cdr D Crowley Milling DFC*	4/43 to 9/43
Wg Cdr R T P Davidson DFC	9/43 to 1/44
Wg Cdr C L Green DFC	1/44 to 8/44
Wg Cdr W Pitt-Brown DFC	8/44 to 11/44
Wg Cdr M T Judd AFC DFC	11/44 to 2/45
Wg Cdr J G Keep DFC	2/45 to (5/45)

Squadrons

245	(6/43) to (May 45)
174	1/7/43 to 21/1/44 (to APC Eastchurch)
	4/4/44 to 10/11/44 (to APC Warmwell)
	21/11/44 to 8/4/45 (disbanded)
175	1/7/43 to 24/2/44 (to APC Eastchurch)

	8/3/44 to 21/11/44 (to APC Warmwell)
	4/12/44 to (5/45)
184	14/7/44 to 4/12/44 (to APC Warmwell)
	18/12/44 to 7/5/45 (to APC Warmwell)

No 123 Airfield/Wing

Formed for Exercise *Spartan*, it became part of No 35 Wing in April 1943 and transferred to the TAF with that wing (but based at Gatwick) on 1 June 1943 to support Mustang I fighter reconnaissance units. The Airfield was transferred to No 20 Wing, No 84 Group, at Manston on 27 February 1944, taking on a new role with Typhoon squadrons.

Manston	27/2/44
Thorney Island	1/4/44
Funtington	17/6/44
B10	1/7/44
B7	18/7/44
B23	3/9/44
B35	6/9/44
B53	13/9/44
B67	30/10/44
B77	24/11/44
A84	31/12/44
B77	26/1/45
B91	22/3/45
B103	18/4/45

Commanding Officers

| Wg Cdr (later Grp Capt) D J Scott DSO OBE DFC* | 4/44 to 2/45 |
| Grp Capt J R Baldwin DSO* DFC* | 2/45 to (5/45) |

Wing Commanders Flying

Wg Cdr R E P Brooker DFC*	5/44 to 7/44
Wg Cdr W Dring DSO DFC	7/44 to 1/45
	(KIFA 13/1/45)
Wg Cdr C J C Button DSO DFC	1/45 to (5/45)

Squadrons

198	4/3/44 to 17/3/44 (to No 146 Airfield)
	6/4/44 to 22/4/44 (to APC Llanbedr)
	30/4/44 to 6/11/44 (to APC Fairwood Common)
	21/11/44 to (5/45)
609	4/3/44 to 16/3/44 (to No 146 Airfield)
	1/4/44 to 22/4/44 (to APC Llanbedr)
	30/4/44 to (5/45)
183	15/3/44 to 11/4/44 (to APC Llanbedr)
	22/4/44 to 29/4/44 (to No 136 Airfield)
	26/7/44 to (5/45)
197	15/3/44 to 1/4/44 (to No 146 Airfield)
164	3/4/44 to 29/4/44 (to No 136 Airfield)
	26/7/44 to (5/45)

No 124 Airfield/Wing

Formed in Exercise *Spartan*, the Airfield joined No 83 Group in April 1943, moving to Appledram the day after the TAF came into existence, along with its three Typhoon squadrons.

Lasham	(6/43)
Appledram	2/6/43
New Romney	2/7/43
Merston	9/10/43
Odiham	31/12/43
Merston	13/1/44
Hurn	1/4/44

B6	16/6/44
B30	30/8/44
B48	3/9/44
B58	6/9/44
B78	23/9/44
B86	9/1/45
B106	10/4/45
B112	13/4/45
B120	17/4/45
B156	30/4/45
B158	7/5/45

Commanding Officers

Wg Cdr L A Lynn DFC	6/43
Wg Cdr V E Maxwell	6/43 to 8/43
Wg Cdr B G Carroll	9/43 to 7/44
Grp Capt C H Appleton CBE DSO DFC	7/44 to 8/44
	(KIA 12/8/44)
Grp Capt C L Green DSO DFC	8/44 to 12/44
Grp Capt E R Bitmead DFC	1/45 to (5/45)

Wing Commanders Flying

Wg Cdr D E Gillam DSO DFC* AFC	7/43 to 8/43
Wg Cdr A Ingle DFC AFC	8/43 to 9/43
Wg Cdr D R Walker DFC	8/43 to 1/44
Wg Cdr E Haabjorn DFC	1/44 to 8/44
Wg Cdr C D North-Lewis DSO DFC*	8/44 to 4/45
Wg Cdr G F H Webb DFC*	4/45 to 5/45
	(KIA 2/5/44)
Wg Cdr M R Ingle-Finch DFC AFC	5/45 to (5/45)

Squadrons

175	(6/43) to 1/7/43 (to No 121 Airfield)
181	(6/43) to 6/2/44 (to APC Eastchurch)
	21/2/44 to 12/1/45
	3/2/45 to (5/45)
182	(6/43) to 5/1/44 (to APC Eastchurch)
	23/1/44 to 3/2/45 (to APC Warmwell)
	21/2/45 to (5/45)
247	10/7/43 to 1/4/44 (to APC Eastchurch)
	24/4/44 to 21/2/45 (to APC Warmwell)
	7/3/45 to (5/45)
137	13/8/44 to 7/3/45 (to APC Warmwell)
	19/3/45 to (5/45)

No 129 Airfield/Wing

Formed at Gatwick on 4 July 1943 under the control of No 39 (Reconnaissance) Wing to support tactical reconnaissance Mustang I units. In April 1944 changed role to support Typhoon fighter-bomber operations, but disbanded on 14 July 1944.

Odiham	2/4/44
Westhampnett	22/4/44
In transit	13/6/44
B10	28/6/44

Commanding Officer

| Wg Cdr D S C Macdonald DFC | 2/44 to 7/44 |

Squadron

184 (Typhoon IB)   3/4/44 to 14/7/44 (to No 121 Wing)

No 136 Airfield/Wing

Formed at Fairlop on 22 November 1943 to support Hurricane and Typhoon squadrons under the control of No 20 Wing, No 84 Group. Disbanded on 30 July 1944 during reorganisation of 2nd TAF.

Fairlop	22/11/43
Thorney Island	15/3/44
Llanbedr	9/4/44
Thorney Island	29/4/44
Old Sarum	2/5/44
Thorney Island	6/5/44
Funtington	17/6/44
Hurn	22/6/44

Commanding Officers
Wg Cdr J I Kilmartin DFC	11/43 to 7/44

Wing Commanders Flying
Wg Cdr B Drake DSO, DFC*	11/43 to 4/44
Wg Cdr J M Bryan DFC*	5/44 to 6/44
	(KIA 10/6/44)
Wg Cdr W Dring DFC	6/44 to 7/44

Squadrons
164	22/11/43 to 4/1/44 (to Twinwood Farm)
	14/1/44 to 11/2/44 (to Twinwood Farm/Acklington)
	15/3/44 to 22/4/44 (to No 123 Airfield)
	28/4/44 to 17/7/44 (to No 123 Wing)
195	22/11/43 to 15/2/44 (disbanded)
193	20/2/44 to 6/4/44 (to APC Llanbedr/No 146 Airfield)
183	11/4/44 to 22/4/44 (at APC Llanbedr, to No 123 Airfield)
	29/4/44 to 14/7/44 (to APC Eastchurch/No 123 Wing)
198	22/4/44 to 28/4/44 (at APC Llanbedr)
609	22/4/44 to 28/4/44 (at APC Llanbedr)
266	13/7/44 to 20/7/44 (to No 146 Wing)
263	17/7/44 to 23/7/44 (to APC and No 146 Wing)

No 143 (RCAF) Airfield/Wing

Formed 10 January 1944 at Ayr to control three RCAF Typhoon squadrons assigned to No 22 Sector.

Ayr	10/1/44
Hurn	18/3/44
Funtington	2/4/44
Hurn	20/4/44
In transit	18/6/44
B9	26/6/44
B24	30/8/44
B48	3/9/44
B58	6/9/44
B78	21/9/44
B100	29/3/45
B108	9/4/45
B110	12/4/45
B150	19/4/45

Commanding Officers
Wg Cdr F W Hillock	1/44 to 7/44
Grp Capt P Y Davoud OBE DSO DFC	7/44 to 12/44
Grp Capt A D Nesbitt DFC	1/45 to (5/45)

Wing Commanders Flying
Wg Cdr R Marples DFC	1/44 to 1/44

Wg Cdr R T P Davidson DFC	1/44 to 5/44
Wg Cdr M T Judd DFC AFC	5/44 to 10/44
Wg Cdr F G Grant DSO DFC	10/44 to (5/45)

Squadrons
438	10/1/44 to 22/5/44 (to APC Llanbedr)
	29/5/44 to 19/3/45 (to Warmwell APC)
	3/4/45 to (5/45)
439	10/1/44 to 11/5/44 (to Hutton Cranswick APC)
	20/5/44 to 3/4/45
	22/4/45 to (5/45)
440	8/2/44 to 22/4/45 (to Warmwell APC)
	8/5/45 to (5/45)
168	2/10/44 to 26/2/45 (disbanded)

No 146 Airfield/Wing

Formed at Tangmere on 31 January 1944 to support Typhoon fighter-bomber squadrons under the control of No 20 Wing, in No 11 Group, ADGB. Transferred to No 84 Group, 2nd TAF, on 10 March 1944.

Tangmere	31/1/44
Needs Oar Point	10/4/44
Hurn	3/7/44
B15	8/8/44
B3	19/7/44
B23	5/9/44
B37	7/9/44
	(air element at Manston)
B51	11/9/44
B70	1/10/44
B89	14/2/45
B105	17/4/45
B111	30/4/45

Commanding Officers
Wg Cdr E W W Ellis	2/44 to 7/44
Grp Capt D E Gillam DSO** DFC* AFC	7/44 to 2/45
Grp Capt J C Wells DFC**	2/45 to (5/45)

Wing Commanders Flying
Wg Cdr D E Gillam DSO DFC* AFC	2/44 to 3/44
Wg Cdr E R Baker DFC	4/44 to 6/44
	(KIA 16/6/44)
Wg Cdr J R Baldwin DFC	6/44 to 11/44
Wg Cdr J C Wells DFC*	11/44 to 2/45
Wg Cdr J H Deall DSO DFC	2/45 to (5/45)

Squadrons
183	(3/44) to 15/3/44
197	(3/44) to 15/3/44 (to No 123 Airfield)
	1/4/44 to 25/11/44 (to APC Fairwood Common)
	12/12/44 to (5/45)
257	(3/44) to 11/4/44 (to APC Fairwood Common)
	12/4/44 to 11/8/44 (to APC Fairwood Common)
	30/8/44 to 5/3/45 (disbanded)
609	16/3/44 to 1/4/44 (to No 123 Airfield)
198	16/3/44 to 30/3/44 (to APC Llanbedr and No 123 Airfield)
266	22/3/44 to 27/4/44 (to Snaith for smoke-laying exercise)
	6/5/44 to 29/6/44 (to APC Eastchurch and No 136 Wing)
	20/7/44 to 25/4/45 (to APC Fairwood Common)
193	11/4/44 to 18/9/44 (to APC Fairwood Common)
	6/10/44 to (5/45)
263	5/8/44 to 13/1/45 (to APC Fairwood Common)
	10/2/45 to (5/45)

APPENDIX 2

NUMBERED AIRFIELDS

The following airfields were occupied by Typhoon wings in France (Fr), Belgium (Be), Holland (Nl) and Germany (Gr) between June 1944 and September 1945

A84 Chievres, Be	B23 Morainville, Fr	B67 Ursel, Be	B106 Twente, Nl
B2 Bazenville, Fr	B24 St-Andre-de-l'Eure, Fr	B70 Antwerp/Deurne, Be	B108 Rheine, Gr
B3 Ste-Croix-sur-Mer, Fr	B30 Fresnoy-Folny, Fr	B77 Gilze-Rijen, Nl	B110 Achmer, Gr
B4 Beny-sur-Mer, Fr	B35 Baromesnil, Fr	B78 Eindhoven, Nl	B111 Ahlhorn, Gr
B5 Le Fresne-Camilly, Fr	B37 Corry, Fr	B80 Volkel, Nl	B112 Hopsten, Gr
B6 Coulombs, Fr	B42 Beauvais-Tille, Fr	B86 Helmond, Nl	B120 Wunstorf, Gr
B7 Martragny, Fr	B48 Amiens-Glisy, Fr	B89 Mill, Nl	B150 Hustedt, Gr
B8 Sommervieu, Fr	B50 Vitry-en-Artois, Fr	B91 Kluis, Nl	B156 Luneburg, Gr
B9 Lantheuil, Fr	B51 Lille/Vendeville, Fr	B100 Goch, Gr	B158 Lubeck, Gr
B10 Plumetot, Fr	B53 Merville, Fr	B103 Plantlunne, Gr	
B15 Ryes, Fr	B58 Melsbroek, Be	B105 Drope, Gr	

COLOUR PLATES

Notes

All the Typhoon illustrations in this section are based on contemporary photographs taken in 1943-45, although not all of the latter appear in this publication for space or quality reasons. All Typhoons in the 2nd TAF wore the same basic camouflage scheme – uppersurfaces in a disruptive pattern of Dark Green and Ocean Grey, with Medium Sea Grey undersides. However, weathering, repainting after repair and varying paint supplies produced differences in the basic colours, and this has been represented to some degree by variations in the colours depicted in these profiles. Of particular note are the Typhoons that operated in the extremely dusty conditions in Normandy. After just one day based at B2 Bazenville, No 184 Sqn's Flg Off Ian Handyside wrote in the unit's unofficial diary that the 'the green camouflage of the Typhoon was changed to a browny desert colour'. Colours of personal markings are, in most cases, not known, so those shown here are speculative in nature.

Aircraft illustrated with serial numbers earlier than MN306 had three-blade propellers and the original small tailplane, whilst those between MN306 and MN600 had the larger, 'Tempest' tailplane, but were still fitted with three-bladed propellers (unless noted otherwise). Aircraft with serial number MN601 or later had four-bladed propellers and 'Tempest' tailplanes.

1

Typhoon IB R8871/EL-G of No 181 Sqn, No 124 Airfield, Merston, June 1943
One of No 181 Sqn's original Typhoon bombers, having been delivered to Duxford on 16 October 1942, R8871 was usually flown by Plt Off Ted Haddock and carried the name *CEMETERY BAIT II* just forward of the cockpit. Haddock was shot down in R8866 on 15 July 1943, and following a lengthy evasion aided by the Resistance and capture and ill-treatment by the Gestapo, he survived as a PoW. *CEMETERY BAIT II* was one of dozens of Typhoons that were broken down for spares by repair contractors Taylorcraft during August 1943.

2

Typhoon IB JP496/RD of No 121 Airfield, Westhampnett, October 1943
Wg Cdr R T P Davidson was promoted from CO of No 175 Sqn to wing commander flying No 121 Airfield in September 1943, at which point he had the codes HH-W on his Typhoon JP496 replaced by his abbreviated initials R-D. The aircraft carried one German, two Italian and two Japanese kill markings, and it probably had a second swastika added after he shared in the destruction of a LeO 451 transport aircraft on 8 January 1944. Davidson transferred to No 143 Wing RCAF a short while later, taking JP496 with him, but it was eventually replaced by MN518 in April 1944. JP496 was then despatched to Cunliffe-Owen for modification, later seeing service with No 3 Tactical Exercise Unit (TEU) and No 56 OTU.

3

Typhoon IB JP649/ZY-Z of No 247 Sqn, No 124 Airfield, Merston, November 1943
When Erik Haabjorn took command of No 247 Sqn in late August 1943, he adopted JP649 as Z, his personal aircraft. The squadron started flying bomber operations in early November of that same year, and Haabjorn flew the aircraft until the beginning of January 1944, when it was replaced

by a new Z, JR449, fitted with a sliding hood. JP649 was re-coded H and lost on a long-range sweep to Chateaudun on 14 February 1944. Its pilot, Flg Off A S Aitchison, was killed.

4
Typhoon IB JP648/JE-D of No 195 Sqn, No 136 Wing, Fairlop, December 1943
This aircraft was normally flown by Flg Off Ken Trott (whose *Popeye* marking it carried on the engine air intake) from late August 1943 to January 1944. During the latter two months the unit was operating from No 136 Airfield, Fairlop, mainly engaged in attacking *Noball* sites. At the beginning of February No 195 Sqn's Typhoons were transferred to No 164 Sqn, and later in the month the unit was formally disbanded. JP648 went on to see service with No 257 Sqn, before being damaged when a tyre burst on take-off. Following repair, the aircraft flew with No 3 TEU and No 55 OTU.

5
Typhoon IB JP510/FM-Y of No 257 Sqn, No 146 Wing, Tangmere, March 1944
Having served with No 257 Sqn as FM-A, Sqn Ldr Fokes' JP510 (see pages 26 and 37 of *Osprey Aircraft of the Aces 27 – Typhoon and Tempest Aces of World War 2*) went to Hawker at Langley for canopy and RP modifications in January 1944. When it was returned to No 257 Sqn in early March, the unit was about to join No 146 Airfield. Re-coded FM-Y, it still retained Sqn Ldr Fokes' pennant, personal marking and code letter A on the nose, although he was now flying a new A, MN118. JP510 was lost on operations on 16 March 1944 when it suffered engine failure over France. Its pilot, Plt Off J B Wood, was captured.

6
Typhoon IB JP535/XP-A of No 174 Sqn, No 121 Wing, Holmsley South, April 1944
One of the first No 174 Sqn Typhoons to be fitted with RP rails, JP535 had served with the unit from July 1943. Flown by many different pilots, but frequently by Flg Off Harry Markby RAAF in the winter months (including the escort mission for the Amiens prison attack on 18 February 1944), the aircraft was also flown on No 174 Sqn's first successful RP sorties on 9 February 1944. After modifications by Cunliffe Owen in May it flew with No 245 Sqn, before being lost to flak on operations with No 184 Sqn on 21 February 1945. JP535's pilot, Flt Lt K A Creamer, was captured.

7
Typhoon IB JR132/F3-F of No 438 Sqn RCAF, No 143 Wing RCAF, Hurn, April 1944
One of five Typhoons transferred from No 186 to No 438 Sqn when the former equipped with Spitfires in February 1944, JR132 was part of No 438 Sqn's initial equipment, but it was flown to Cunliffe Owen for modifications in early May 1944. Subsequently, the aircraft flew with No 3 TEU and

No 55 OTU prior to being scrapped in June 1945. It is seen here fitted with an M10 smoke tank.

8
Typhoon IB MN463/OV of No 197 Sqn, No 146 Wing, Needs Oar Point, May 1944
No 197 Sqn's commanding officer, Sqn Ldr Don Taylor, chose to identify his personal aircraft by applying just the squadron code letters OV, and no individual letter. Taylor finished his operational tour in July, whereupon the aircraft became OV-M and it was usually flown by Flt Sgt 'Paddy' Byrne. MN463 was lost with its pilot, Flt Sgt L S Bell, during Falaise Gap operations on 18 August 1944.

9
Typhoon IB MN454/HF-S of No 183 Sqn, No 136 Wing, Thorney Island, May 1944
Delivered to No 183 Sqn whilst at Llanbedr APC on 13 April 1944, MN454 was adopted by the unit's commanding officer, Sqn Ldr The Honourable Felix Scarlett. On 3 May MN454 was flown to Northolt for an inspection of the latest aircraft types and weapons by King George VI. Eight days later the aircraft was damaged by flak and fire, but after repair it was allocated to No 164 Sqn. MN454 was shot down by Fw 190s on D-Day with the loss of its pilot, Flg Off A E Roberts.

10
Typhoon IB MN666/CG of No 121 Wing, Holmsley South, June 1944
After an 'Air Test' on 20 May 1944, MN666 was adopted by Wg Cdr Charles Green as his personal aircraft – he used it to lead the first RP attack at H-Hour +20 on D-Day. It appears that Green later operated three other CGs while leading No 121 Wing in Normandy. By 20 July MN666 was with No 3501 SU at Cranfield, from where it was issued to the FLS at Milfield on 17 September 1944. The FLS was absorbed by the Central Fighter Establishment late in 1944 and MN666, stripped of its camouflage and known as 'the Silver Bullet', was used by instructors on FLS courses.

11
Typhoon IB MN353/HH-J of No 175 Sqn, No 121 Wing, Holmsley South, June 1944
Flt Lt 'V-J' Vernon Jarvis, 'A' Flight commander, flew this aircraft from late April 1944 through to the beginning of July, when it was replaced by MN856. MN353 subsequently became HH-U. Declared 'Cat B' in September, it was repaired by Taylorcraft and eventually saw service with No 266 Sqn as ZH-J in April 1945. The aircraft was destroyed in a forced landing on 8 July 1945.

12
Typhoon IB MN630/PR-B of No 609 Sqn, No 123 Wing, Thorney Island, June 1944
Brand new when flown on D-Day by Flt Lt E R A Roberts in an attack on the 'coastwatcher' (radar) at Le Havre, MN630 flew on operations until 12 August 1944 when it was written off in a ground

collision with another Typhoon at B7 Martragny. The spinner colour is speculative, but it is known that a number of No 609 Sqn aircraft had coloured spinners (including red) immediately prior to the D-Day invasion.

13
Typhoon IB MN601/MR-K of No 245 Sqn, No 121 Wing, Holmsley South, June 1944

The Typhoon in which Flg Off Bill Smith made the first wheels down landing on the first RAF ALG in the Normandy beachhead, MN601 had only been delivered to No 245 Sqn just days before. The fighter continued in service with the unit until damaged in action on 31 July 1944, after which it was repaired and then allocated to No 263 Sqn. In March 1945 MN601 was overhauled by Marshall of Cambridge, but saw no further service. It was sold for scrap in 1947 but, reputedly, a wing from this aircraft was part of the last (composite) Typhoon airframe scrapped in the UK, at No 60 MU Rufforth, in 1955.

14
Typhoon IB MN529/BR-N of No 184 Sqn, No 129 Wing, Westhampnett and B2 Bazenville, June 1944

MN529 was received by No 184 Sqn at the end of May 1944 and allocated to Flg Off Ian Handyside. It was the squadron's practice to mark unit code letters forward of the roundel on both sides of the fuselage, so when D-Day stripes were applied, individual code letters were obliterated. They were subsequently repainted on the fin unusually large, and overlapping the fin flash. This aircraft boasted a four-bladed propeller. See the note at the head of this appendix regarding the colour of this machine. MN529 later served with No 193 Sqn until it blew up while attacking gun positions at Breskens on 12 October 1944, killing its pilot, Flt Sgt R A Pratt.

15
Typhoon IB MN413/I8-T of No 440 Sqn RCAF, No 143 Wing RCAF, B9 Lantheuil, July 1944

Allocated to No 438 Sqn shortly before D-Day, MN413 was transferred to No 440 Sqn in July and initially coded F, then T. On 1 August 1944 Flt Sgt N L Gordon made a belly-landing at B9 when the undercarriage failed to lock. The resulting damage was declared 'Cat B' and MN413 was transported to the UK for repair by Marshall of Cambridge. Returned to service in March 1945, MN413 flew with No 184 Sqn as BR-K and was scrapped at Dunsfold when the unit disbanded.

16
Typhoon IB JR438/EL-W of No 181 Sqn, No 124 Wing, B6 Coulombs, July 1944

One of the first production Typhoons with a sliding hood, JR438 served with No 137 Sqn before going to No 13 MU at Henlow for RP modifications in May 1944. In June it was sent to No 181 Sqn, becoming Flg Off Jack Rendall's aircraft, and the Typhoon remained in service until shot down by flak on 24 February 1945 – Sgt A P Mann was killed.

17
Typhoon IB MN798/XM-Y of No 182 Sqn, No 124 Wing, B6 Coulombs, July 1944

After brief service with No 247 Sqn, MN798 was transferred to No 182 Sqn (probably after an engine change following the 'retreat' from Normandy to Hurn). Coded Y, it was the last of Flg Off Douglas Coxhead's Ys before he finished his first tour. MN798 was written off after being hit by flak and making a forced landing in Allied territory on 15 December 1944.

18
Typhoon IB MN600/ZH-A of No 266 Sqn, No 146 Wing, B3 St Croix, August 1944

Entering service with No 266 Sqn in the week before D-Day, MN600 survived until 9 August 1944, when it was shot down by flak – Flt Sgt P C Green evaded. The small serial number on the fin is a remnant from the period when the larger serial number was partly obscured by D-Day stripes.

19
Typhoon IB MN941/DJS of No 123 Wing, B53 Merville, September 1944

Marked with his initials, MN941 was flown by Grp Capt Desmond Scott, commanding officer of No 123 Wing between July and 10 December 1944, when the aircraft was transferred to No 183 Sqn. It was shot down by flak on 22 February 1945, with the loss of its South African pilot, Capt A Lens.

20
Typhoon IB MN925/OV-Z of No 197 Sqn, No 146 Wing, B51 Lille-Vendeville, September 1944

Delivered to No 197 Sqn in early August 1944, MN925 was usually flown by Flt Sgt Derek Tapson until mid-December when it was transferred to No 413 RSU. After repair the aircraft was allocated in January 1945 to No 193 Sqn, with whom it remained until the unit disbanded at the end of August 1945.

21
Typhoon IB MN951/TP-A of No 198 Sqn, No 123 Wing, B53 Merville, September 1944

Having lost his previous A to flak damage, Flt Lt Denis Sweeting (the commander of No 198 Sqn's 'A' Flight) took over MN951 'K' as his new 'A'. It was named *The Uninvited* after the 1943 Hollywood film – a ghost story. Sweeting finished his operational tour in January 1945, but MN951 soldiered on with the unit until July of that year, when it was hit in its dispersal by another Typhoon.

22
Typhoon IB MP189/KN-L of No 124 Wing, B78 Eindhoven, September 1944

Delivered to No 181 Sqn at the end of August 1944

and adopted by Wg Cdr Kit North-Lewis to replace his MN922, which was hit by flak on 26 August, MP189 was flown on 40 operational sorties as KN-L before being damaged whilst North-Lewis was on leave in early December. After repair by No 403 RSU, MP189 was allocated to No 247 Sqn as Sqn Ldr B G Stapleton's aircraft. He first flew the aircraft on 22 December, but was shot down in it the following day and captured.

23
Typhoon IB JP504/SF-R of No 137 Sqn, No 124 Wing, B78 Eindhoven, October 1944
After initial service with No 197 Sqn as Sqn Ldr 'Jacko' Holmes' OV-Z, and modifications at Hawker, JP504 suffered engine failure and a wheels-up landing whilst with No 83 GSU. Following repairs by Taylorcraft, JP504 was issued to No 137 Sqn and usually flown by Flg Off Ken Brain, coded SF-R. Hit by flak three times on 7 November, it was replaced by PD611. Repaired at No 403 RSU and returned to No 137 Sqn as E, JP504 was shot down by flak and WO W A Flett killed on 26 December 1944.

24
Typhoon IB MN716/F3-A of No 438 Sqn RCAF, No 143 Wing RCAF, B78 Eindhoven, October 1944
Delivered to No 439 Sqn in early June, MN716 was soon transferred to No 438 Sqn. Battle damage on 23 January 1945 meant a visit to an RSU, but the fighter was back with No 438 Sqn at the beginning of March and remained with the unit until it was disbanded at the end of August 1945. MN716 was then flown to No 83 Group Disbandment Centre (GDC) at Dunsfold and scrapped a few weeks later.

25
Typhoon IB PD600/DP-C of No 193 Sqn, No 146 Wing, B70 Deurne, November 1944
American Flg Off Roy Heath flew this unusually marked aircraft, nicknamed *LITTLE RAE*, in November-December 1944. It also had his name in script beneath the starboard canopy sill. Heath wore an Eighth Air Force B-17 waist gunner's helmet when on operations! Damaged by German fighters on Christmas Day 1944, PD600 was declared 'Cat B' and repaired by Taylorcraft, but it saw no further service.

26
Typhoon IB EK140/QC-K of No 168 Sqn, No 143 Wing RCAF, B78 Eindhoven, December 1944
After service with No 59 OTU and the FLS as MF-X, EK140 was modified by Cunliffe Owen in May 1944 and eventually allocated to No 168 Sqn on the day the unit flew its first Typhoon operation, 12 October 1944. When No 168 Sqn disbanded, it was transferred to No 245 Sqn at the beginning of April 1945 and then to No 247 Sqn two months later. EK140 was one of the last Typhoons in service with an operational unit, and it was scrapped after a forced landing (caused by an overspeeding engine) at Aldermaston on 12 September 1945.

27
Typhoon IB RB205/FGG of No 143 Wing RCAF, B78 Eindhoven, December 1944
Although officially allocated to No 440 Sqn, RB205 was adopted by Wg Cdr F G Grant as his personal aircraft on 26 October 1944. Damaged by flak on 24 December, it was despatched to No 403 RSU (also at Eindhoven) for repair, only to be destroyed by strafing Luftwaffe fighters during the *Bodenplatte* attack on New Year's Day 1945.

28
Typhoon IB MN345/5V-G of No 439 Sqn RCAF, No 143 Wing RCAF, B78 Eindhoven, December 1944
Delivered to No 438 Sqn in late April 1944, MN345 was coded F3-D. One of five Typhoons from the unit to be damaged by flak on D-Day, it was repaired by a working party from No 419 RSU. By late August MN345 was with No 439 Sqn, coded G and adopted by Flg Off J A Brown, who named it after his hometown, Peace River. The aircraft's black and white spinner was just one of a number of asymmetric styles favoured by No 439 Sqn with the intention of distracting German flak gunners. In this case it clearly did not work, as Brown was shot down in MN345 on 6 November 1944. He survived as a PoW.

29
Typhoon IB MP126/ZY-Y of No 247 Sqn, No 124 Wing, B78 Eindhoven, December 1944
Delivered to No 247 Sqn at the end of August 1944, MP126 was adopted by Sqn Ldr Basil G Stapleton as his personal aircraft – it carried a symbolic painting of a rocket smashing the Third Reich. Heavy losses depleted the squadron's reserves of serviceable Typhoons in December, and on the 5th of the month Dutch pilot Plt Off 'Frickie' Wiersum borrowed Sqn Ldr Stapleton's 'kite' for a sortie to the Munster area, only to be shot down by flak near Bocholt. He too survived as a PoW.

30
Typhoon IB MN987/DP-T of No 193 Sqn, No 146 Wing, B70 Deurne, December 1944
This long-serving Typhoon was the usual mount of Flg Off Mike Bulleid, one of 2nd TAF's more successful Typhoon pilots in aerial combat post-D-Day. Two small swastikas can be seen just below the windscreen. The aircraft was transferred to No 193 Sqn at the end of August 1944 and MN987 served with the unit until it was disbanded in August 1945. The Typhoon was eventually scrapped at Kemble-based No 5 MU in September 1946.

31
Typhoon IB R7620/XP-P of No 174 Sqn, No 121 Wing, B80 Volkel, February 1945
Plt Off Frank Wheeler usually flew MN810/XP-Y, but on 22 February 1945 his usual mount was not available. Instead, Wheeler flew P on an 'armed

recce' to Osnabruck. This latter aircraft was R7620, newly arrived on the squadron, but the oldest Typhoon to see action in 1945. It had flown with No 56 Sqn in early 1942 as US-G, then spent time with de Havilland on propeller trials in 1943, after which it had been rebuilt (probably by Taylorcraft). RPs are omitted from the illustration to show the tropical air filter as installed on rebuilt Typhoons from the last quarter of 1944 onwards. Hit by flak, R7620 was crash-landed by Wheeler at Volkel and damaged beyond repair.

32

Typhoon IB MN978/FJ-Z of No 164 Sqn, No 123 Wing, B77 Gilze-Rijen, February 1945

Sqn Ldr Van Lierde (one of the few Typhoon aces, and top scorer by day against V1 flying bombs) took command of No 164 Sqn in August 1944, adopting MN978 as his FJ-Z – he had previously flown Tempests marked JF-Z with No 56 Sqn. Van Lierde flew Z in 49 of the 69 operational sorties that he completed during his tour with No 164 Sqn. MN978 was damaged by enemy action on 26 February 1945 and repaired by Taylorcraft, although it saw no further service prior to being scrapped at Kemble in 1946.

33

Typhoon IB RB232/HE-O of No 263 Sqn, No 146 Wing, B89 Mill, March 1945

Delivered to No 263 Sqn in December 1944, RB232 was allocated to Plt Off John Shellard, replacing his previous HE-O, MN404 (likewise named *Kitty*). Suffering minor battle damage on 19 April 1945, this aircraft would normally have been repaired but the end of the war brought early scrapping in June 1945.

34

Typhoon IB MP197/MR-U of No 245 Sqn, No 121 Wing, B80 Volkel, March 1945

Joining No 245 Sqn in August 1944, MP197 was with No 412 RSU before the end of the month. After repair, it was returned to No 245 Sqn and coded U. The aircraft duly remained with the unit until it was disbanded in August 1945. At some unknown time in its career with No 245 Sqn (but during hostilities), MP197 acquired what is believed to be a unique marking on a Typhoon – a 'sharksmouth'. It had been flown in late 1944/early 1945 by Flt Lt H T 'Moose' Mossip RCAF until he was killed in action in another aircraft on 7 March 1945. MP197 then became Sqn Ldr Tony Zweigbergk's mount. The colours of the mouth marking are not known for certain, with red being the most likely colour for the interior.

35

Typhoon IB SW460/MR-Z of No 245 Sqn, No 121 Wing, B150 Hustedt, April 1945

'B' Flight commander Flt Lt Geoff Murphy usually flew MR-Z, and his last Typhoon so marked (thought to be SW460, although it may possibly have been SW560) carried artwork illustrating Z from the spoof phonetic alphabet – Zed for breezes/zephyr breezes.

36

Typhoon IB RB326/5V-V of No 439 Sqn RCAF, No 143 Wing RCAF, B150 Hustedt, April 1945

Flown by No 439 Sqn from January 1945 until the unit was disbanded at the end of August, RB326 was last reported with No 83 GDC at Dunsfold on 31 August 1945, and it was probably scrapped there. Most of the squadron's aircraft had their individual letters repeated on the nose cowling – a style unique to No 439 Sqn among operational Typhoon units.

37

Typhoon IB RB273/DP-E of No 193 Sqn, No 146 Wing, B105 Drope, April 1945

After brief service with No 257 Sqn and repair by No 423 RSU, RB273 joined No 193 Sqn and was adopted by 'A' Flight commander Flt Lt J G Simpson as his *Norma VII* just before his tour finished. New 'A' Flight commander Flt Lt David Ince took over RB273, flying operational napalm bomb trials in it as shown in this illustration. Indeed, he performed several demonstration drops with the aircraft after the war.

38

Typhoon IB SW493/DP-S of No 193 Sqn, No 146 Wing, B89 Mill, April 1945

Sqn Ldr Don 'Butch' Taylor commanded three Typhoon units, namely Nos 195, 197 and finally 193 Sqns. SW493 was the last of his Typhoons, and it was named *BETTY X*. Post-war, it would be painted with red trim, adorned with the squadron badge and renamed plain *BETTY*. In April 1945 SW493 was filmed being loaded with supply canisters (as illustrated) that were to be dropped at a pre-arranged location for SAS troops operating behind the German lines.

39

Typhoon IB RB431/JCB of No 123 Wing, B103 Plantlunne, April 1945

Although on charge with No 609 Sqn, RB431 was routinely used by Wg Cdr J C Button as *ZIPP XI* (his personal cine-camera equipped aircraft) in the last two months of the war. It was eventually scrapped at No 51 MU in March 1946.

40

Typhoon IB SW496/JB of No 123 Wing, B103 Plantlunne, April 1945

One of two Typhoons available to Grp Capt J R Baldwin when OC No 123 Wing in the last months of the war, SW496 was equipped to carry bombs – his other similarly marked aircraft, SW470, was configured for RPs. Shortly after VE Day Baldwin relinquished this aircraft, retaining SW470 for his personal use. Allocated to No 198 Sqn, SW496 was damaged in a taxiing accident on 22 July 1945. Repaired and stored at No 51 MU Lichfield, it was eventually scrapped here in 1947.

INDEX

References to illustrations are shown in **bold**. Plate numbers are **bold** followed by page and caption locators in brackets.